Monty Don

Growing

Out of

Trouble

HODDER &
STOUGHTON

Copyright © 2006 by Monty Don

First published in Great Britain in 2006 by Hodder & Stoughton
A division of Hodder Headline

The right of Monty Don to be identified as the Author
of the Work has been asserted by him in accordance
with the Copyright, Designs and Patents Act 1988.

A Hodder & Stoughton book

2

By arrangement with the BBC
The BBC logo is a registered trademark of the British Broadcasting
Corporation and is used under licence
BBC logo © BBC 1996

The author wishes to thank the *Guardian* and the *Hereford Times*
for their permission to reproduce extracts.

A CIP catalogue record for this title is available from the British Library

ISBN 978 0 340 89847 5
ISBN 0 340 89847 X

Typeset in Sabon by Hewer Text UK Ltd, Edinburgh
Printed and bound by Clays Ltd, St Ives plc

Hodder Headline's policy is to use papers that are natural, renewable
and recyclable products and made from wood grown in sustainable
forests. The logging and manufacturing processes are expected to
conform to the environmental regulations of the country of origin.

Hodder & Stoughton Ltd
A division of Hodder Headline
338 Euston Road
London NW1 3BH

To all those caught in
the spiral of addiction

Contents

Acknowledgements

I don't like overblown acknowlegements but when you have read this book you will see that many people have been involved and without them the book nor the events it describes would have happened. So many thanks are due. Let's start at the top. David Chantler, the West Mercia Chief Probation Officer, has backed the scheme from the earliest idle thoughts and without doubt has been the single most influential figure in creating the environment and circumstances for it to happen – not least through his passion for good food. It has been inspirational to work with him. He heads a probation service that is under-resourced, overworked, often not much esteemed by the general public and yet doing essential and at times heroic work. In the following pages I am often deeply frustrated by beaurocracy and culture of the institution but I am never less than filled with admiration for the individuals trying to do an impossible job for the greater good of society.

The West Mercia Care Trust backed the project both financially and practically from the outset and have remained true to its methods and ideals. I am greateful to all of them but I would like to especially thank Georgina Britten-Long for unfailingingly practical help.

The BBC were enthusiastic and quick to set up the documentary series which in turn enabled wheels to turn much faster than they otherwise might have done. It has involved thousands of hours of sharing the lives of this group, which they have done with remarkable tact and discretion. Many people were involved in the production, particularly Dee, Butch, Adam and Dan who were all inspirational.

1

In my own set-up Leigh Hughes and in particular Marsha Arnold have done a huge amount of work both for the project and for me. Marsha did most of the research for this book, most of the day-to-day organisation for the project, most of the work setting up the charity and most of the admin to keep my complicated working life running vaguely smoothly. She held it all together and I literally could not have done it without her.

Rupert Lancaster at Hodder has been the most flexible and supportive editor imaginable. This book has broken every publishing rule and its physical existence is a tribute to him. My agent Araminta Whitley has, as ever, supported and guided me and made many useful suggestions to tone and content.

The most important people to thank are the group themselves: Lee, Adam, Wayne, Dean, Tom, All three Chrises, Andy B, Andrés, Katie, Paul, Sam, Steve, Shayne, Chubby, Barrie and Martin. I am proud of what they have achieved and to be associated with them. Then those that worked for and with us: our landlords David and Tricia Reeve who went far, far beyond the call of duty in both supporting and tolerating us as well as providing a home when we badly needed it and bore the lack of gratitude for that with extraordinary good grace and cheerfulness.

Philip Lloyd, Andy Trim and Beth Cohen who worked and advised specifically on the management of the land and stock. Jack Griffiths, and Tony Smith who collected and drove and joined in with a constantly cheerful and paternal goodwill. Jack's wife, Cath Griffiths, who typed up the daybook, which saved me many hours of work, Lou and Gloria who came and volunteered help and selflessly added much. Ray Harris, who provided us with four lovely Tamworth pigs. Kubota Tractors, who loaned us a tractor and range of implements that not only helped enormously in the work but also provided a range of new skills that proved to be important for a number of the group.

By far the biggest thanks however goes to Robert Hudson –

Rocky – who carried us all with strength, grace, wisdom and terrible jokes. He is the hero of this book. Although his wife Ange is not far behind, for helping so competently and unselfishly and putting up with a husband giving so much of his life to his work – and those dreadful jokes . . .

Finally thanks to my family and in particular Sarah for tolerating and supporting this obsessional, consuming and at times crushing things in their lives.

It should be stressed that although all these people and many others have helped and supported me over this book any errors, omissions or false conclusions are mine and mine alone.

Introduction

Whenever I am interviewed about the project invariably the question comes up why? Why did I get involved in all this? I suspect that the journalists are hoping that I will confess to my own heroin addiction that I overcame through the powers of gardening. It would be good copy, and if it were true I would readily admit to it, but I am afraid that there are no such sensational skeletons in my cupboard. Whilst I grew up in a generation that saw drugs as part of an attractive alternative culture I had friends who became heroin addicts and hated what it did to them and came to loathe everything about the drug, although the opium poppies growing in my garden are incredibly beautiful. But my involvement did not start with heroin or crime. It begins with the earth and the natural world we all share.

I know that earth keeps me sane. It cannot be cheated. It is my base reality. Getting back to earth is an absolute starting point from which everything can grow, everything can be possible. I believe that a close and respectful relationship with the ground we stand upon makes us truer and better people. The details of all our lives are measured in weather and plants and the particular birds that share our patch of ground. It is – or can be – a highly personal, idiosyncratic map that nevertheless can be shared intimately with others. I am equally certain that a society without respect for the natural world, the food it produces or the detail and ritual of the landscape is horribly impoverished.

One of the most banal but powerful symbols of this is a tractor driver with headphones. There are fields near my house belonging to a farmer who is a from a family that has looked after that land for generations. He loves his herd of cattle and tends them expertly. He also has a few acres of arable land that provide straw and feed for the cattle. It is a complex, very modern picture. The arable work, with its hugely expensive heavy machinery used just once or twice a year for specific jobs, is contracted out. Again, very normal and modern. In a nearby field I have counted as many as nine huge tractors harvesting potatoes through the night. At times like these, mercifully rare, living in the country can be like living next to a motorway.

Some of the tractor drivers do not live locally. Many hardly set foot on the land. They drive into the field next door to us with their machinery, do their work and drive away. Whilst they are there, sitting in a comfy chair ten feet above the ground, they have air conditioning and music playing through their head-phones. They hear neither wind nor passing bird. The grime on their hands is much more likely to be engine oil than soil. In short, they do not have any kind of personal relationship with the land that they work. The field only has meaning as a unit of work. The footpath that runs along one side is invariably ploughed up and sown over. The edges of the fields are cultivated up to and including the roots of the hedgerows that bound them so that there is not a scrap of land for local people to walk – let alone mammal, bird or insect to live. The land is reduced to a factory floor.

To understand and care for a piece of land you have to handle it and smell it, feel it stick to your shoes and powder your pockets and silt itself into the creases of your clothes. You have to know the names of the fields and the idiosyncratic character of every one. Accountability and intimacy nurture skill and care.

By the beginning of the twenty-first century the British rural community was undergoing great and damaging changes. The Labour Government that came to power in 1997 neither knew nor cared anything about it. In fact they were rather scared of it and saw the countryside as the natural home of Torydom and a breeding ground for dissent.

Modern politicians are like the huge food companies, centralising and codifying, crushing over the intricacies and subtleties of all that is idiosyncratic and local and particular, with their headphones tuned to central office and their tractors ploughing remorselessly through the footpaths. The message for the past ten years or so has been unambiguous – the countryside does not matter. When they are forced to pay attention to anything rural – foot and mouth disease, fox-hunting, EU subsidies – it is only crisis management. On top of that there seems to have been an attitude of 'New' Labour that all manual work is demeaning and not modern. 'Business' to New Labour is defined by meetings and management targets, not the process of actually producing things.

It is a situation remarkably similar to the Thatcher government's view of the mining community in the early 1980s. Like the miners, what has been left in the wake of this deliberate neglect are villages and towns with the guts ripped out of them, without trades or traditions. There is nothing there for young people to aspire to or hope for. The countryside has become increasingly polarised into large farms relying upon low-paid migrant labour, semi-retired couples whose children have grown up and the traditional workforce with no work, no money and no connection to the land. The small country towns – which still make up a large section of the British population – have few buses to connect them and even fewer trains. If you want a job in the country you need a car and if you want a car you need money from a job. I have known long periods of unemployment as an adult with a family and know how quickly apathy seeps in. Nowhere to go, nothing to do and no money to do it with.

This is where drugs come in. British rural towns have been systematically targeted by drug dealers aiming at this disenfranchised generation. I suppose that this is an example of a successful business. As Rocky, the ex-policeman who runs the group from Worcester that formed the nucleus of this project, said, drugs are just business. In the end it is all down to money.

I was profoundly influenced by a remark that I heard, made by the American farmer and poet Wendell Berry, that you could not start to farm well until you stopped farming for profit. I took that to mean putting the care and husbandry of the land and its many harvests above the monetary profits that might be gained in the short term. This seemed so at odds with all modern food production, indeed all modern business, and yet so patently right that it has been my byword for everything I do since.

Prisons have largely closed down their farming operations because they were 'unprofitable', as though they could be measured in those terms. But you cannot run any farm, smallholding or any growing operation as a business purely on a capitalistic model. It does not work. You end up with hundreds of acres of unregulated polytunnels with growers raising crops under plastic in growing bags filled with material shipped in from the other side of the world and using cheap labour that most certainly is not fair trade whilst pandering to the capricious whims of supermarkets. If that is not your style you cut down millions of hectares of rain forest to grow soya to feed animals in vile conditions, whose carcasses have a few choice cuts selected for cellophane-wrapped display on supermarket shelves and otherwise are ground up for more animal consumption or glue. The capitalist model simply does not meet the sophisticated demands of twenty-first-century food production. The hardworking, honest small farmer struggles to make ends meet and is mocked by the big businesses, governments and consumers.

I was reminded of this when I was talking to one of the huge growers erecting hundreds of acres of polytunnels all over one of the most beautiful stretches of border countryside – 'It's just business,' he said, as if this mindless mantra absolved him of all responsibility for the land, our food culture and thousands of years of rural heritage. Food and farming can never, ever be 'only business'. It is, at the very least, health and education and culture and landscape and the very essence of what we care about and value in life. To reduce food production to profit and loss is a counsel of despair.

Heroin is a perfect metaphor for the alienated, isolated, careless culture that we are evolving. It is no coincidence that 'junk' is one of the many slang names for heroin. Dealers of junk drugs, junk food, junk television, junk religion, junk politics all have their day but there is a terrible price to pay.

It really does not have to be like this. By starting from the ground and tapping into the absolute, uncheatable truth of nature we can make ourselves better. When dealing with plants and animals and the land you cannot be dishonest or fickle. You have to deal with it as it is. That is a good starting point for putting together the pieces of a life. This is not something that can be done second hand. You have to get your own hands dirty.

It seemed obvious to me that anyone lost in addiction, the perpetual crime needed to fund it and the resulting ostracisation that results from repeated conviction, becomes an outlaw without a sense of identity or responsibility to place, community or often even family. To get out of that spiralling trap they must ground themselves in something. In my experience, when it comes to grounding, the earth is as good a place as any to start.

I believe that most people hunger for honesty and truth. This is where nature – even the small patch of humble garden in a back street or housing estate – comes up trumps. With its direct and daily contact with the soil, plants and the seasons, the garden never lies. In its flowing, sinuous shift from weather to weather, season to season and every unfurling stage of its plants, it tells an absolute truth.

The real importance of this is the empowerment that it gives people. If you can grow anything edible, you can step off the seemingly remorseless food treadmill. It is surprising how liberating this is. Once you engage with the simple enough business of feeding yourself with the inevitable attention to weather, season and harvest, it becomes personal. It is about you, your family and friends. Food becomes an aspect of those relationships as well as the intimacy with your plot. I wrote once that every government minister should be obliged to run an allotment. I was deadly serious. It might bring a smattering of honesty into their bunkered, blinkered lives.

Personally I prefer to farm and garden and eat organically, but I would rather have really good non-organic food that is raised and sold locally by people I know than stuff with impeccable organic credentials that has been raised as a purely marketing exercise and distributed in a mass, indiscriminate way. If you know where something has come from and who grew it then food has meaning. The consumer has the power to decide on this. It is our land. We make of it what we eat.

The garden is the best and first place for this to happen. It is beautifully simple and modest. It does not involve pressure groups or big businesses and certainly not governments – just individuals working together in an unstructured but socially responsible and responsive way. With small personal actions, such as growing a few herbs, vegetables or fruit outside the back door, with an unpampered and often unprofitable but often incredibly rich husbandry of land from the smallest back garden to the largest farm we can make ourselves physically, mentally and socially well.

Gardens and gardeners connect right across the country in an unplanned, spontaneous network – not in fact dissimilar to the internet as a model and with the same potential revolutionary power. Gardens are now the front line of the environment, of climate, of food and, I would argue, of some kind of social sanity. I have no illusions that this will change much, but then again it does not have to. Very small is very beautiful.

So – from this simple, domestic, back-garden concept of small, modest action focusing on growing and consuming good organic, local food – the project evolved.

In spring 2004 I was supposed to be making a one-hour film for the BBC about gardening and health. This was stimulated by my own experiences of coping with depression through gardening and working on the land and also the contact that I have had with the charity Thrive that specialises in providing opportunities for people with a range of mental health problems to garden. It works. We all get – and feel – better for being outside and growing things. Looking after something else always results in looking after a part of ourselves. In every sense of the expression, we become better people.

Anyway, the film never got made (we made a film about the garden at Buckingham Palace instead) but I did do a lot of thinking about how far this horticultural health-giving could go and happened to mention that it would be good to get young offenders involved in working on the land as well as people officially 'ill'. The idea was not to take people from prisons but those that the probation service and courts had identified as going off the rails but still open to redemption. I certainly did not want this to be punishment but an opportunity to change things for the better. At very worst it would give a small group the chance to take some exercise outside in the fresh air in a beautiful environment. At best it might offer a chance to change. I have long felt that there is an awful lot of attention on inner cities and their undoubted problems but very little about rural towns and communities. Heroin, with its inevitable accompanying spiral of crime, is a serious problem in small rural towns. Its use is rife. Agriculture offers less and less work for local people even though cheap labour is pouring in from Eastern Europe.

As Felicity Lawrence says in her 2004 Rachel Carson Lecture (which I recommend as essential reading along with her book *Not on the Label*):

Supermarkets keep almost nothing in stock, instead changing their orders to producers by the hour depending on what their barcode scanning tells them they have sold. In this way they can eliminate nearly all financial risk from their end of the chain. The risk is passed down the line, to the farmers, processors and manufacturers who have to increase or decrease their production at short notice, and who therefore want workers they can turn on and off like a tap. The supermarkets are also using their buying power to drive prices down relentlessly. They use the threat of sourcing abroad where it is cheaper – from countries where labour conditions are Dickensian – if British farmers and processors do not oblige. So the farmers and factory owners pass the risk on down the line again to the workers at the bottom. They subcontract their labour to agencies or gang-masters, so that legal responsibility for employment is devolved and pay as little as they can.

One of the many ill-effects of this whole demeaning process is that there is a distinct sense of hopeless disengagement from life amongst young people who would have formerly gone and worked on the land in some capacity. There are few trades or skills to be mastered, few ways to connect and be valued. The middle classes get cheap builders, fruit pickers and cleaners and the working classes get junk food, daytime television and the National Front handing out vile leaflets in the shopping centre. Oh, and heroin.

My idea was passed on to the West Mercia probation service, whose chief probation officer, David Chantler, immediately championed it and took it up with alacrity. It is almost certain that without his initial and sustained involvement this scheme would never have got off the ground.

Then the BBC came on board with a confidence and enthusiasm that was very heartening.

The initial plan was that I would buy a farm and run a kind of agricultural boot camp, but that was clearly too sensational and short-term. I also did not have the necessary money. It seemed better to rent some land and create a smallholding with as varied a range of produce as possible. I met the local Probationary Trust and immediately realised that they had huge experience between them with the assistant chief constable, magistrates, ex-high sheriffs, the chief probation officer and others with years of involvement in this field. They were enthusiastically receptive to the project and we agreed to run it under their auspices with myself as a member of the Trust. They agreed to match the money that I was putting into it and we set about raising more to get us going.

Strictly speaking the project started for Persistent and Priority Offenders. In practice the overlap of this rather clumsily labelled group with drug misuse is at least 80 per cent. (By the by, one of the less savoury aspects of working in an area of government and institutions is the abundance of ugly and vacuous acronyms and titles. It is a world of men in bad suits working flipcharts with oversized print crowing distorted and misleading statistics.) In fact they tend to be referred to as 'Young Offenders' but the term needs clarifying. Technically a 'Young Offender' is someone aged between 10 and 17 who has been convicted of committing a crime. Not one of my group has come from that category. All must be over 18 and there is no upper age limit. In practice all are between 22 and 37 with an average age of about 27. They may not technically be 'young offenders' but most are locked emotionally and in many other ways into the age that they started using heavy drugs – between 13 and 17 – and most have the unnaturally smooth skin and youthful appearance of regular heroin users. To a middle-aged, wrinkled codger like myself they look and seem young, and from any viewpoint they most certainly are offenders.

All my group are on a Drug Treatment and Testing Order

(DTTO). This is specifically designed to wean people off drugs and to be an alternative to prison. The government claims success but the evidence contradicts this. The truth is that no one really knows what to do. The problem is steadily getting worse and no one has come up with any kind of workable solution. Part of the problem is both created and manifested by politics itself. Heroin is a nihilistic, disinterested drug. It seems to me no coincidence that its rise coincides with an age and generation that has little interest or faith in politics. Politicians are generally seen as part of the problem rather than the solution.

This is not to say that the government of the last ten years has not genuinely tried to tackle the drugs problem. They just have not been very successful. There are published reports stating 'tangible improvements' yet all the evidence on the ground is that the situation is getting worse. Inspect the figures and all you see is spin. There is much noise made about the increase in offenders receiving treatment, but where the government claims '75 per cent of those entering treatment in 2004/2005 were retained in or successfully completed programmes', an investigation by the National Audit Office found that more than 70 per cent failed to complete the courses, failed to turn up for tests or training and committed further crimes. It was with this in mind that Rocky, the ex-policeman group mentor, would repeatedly reassure me when I would complain how slow our progress was or how badly things seemed to be going, 'At least they turned up, Mont.' And as a rule, even the most reluctant of them continued to turn up, in foul weather with nothing but the prospect of hard work ahead of them.

I cannot pretend that the lure of growing organic food was the main contributor to their attendance. Most offenders, young or old, have not a clue where their food comes from, what each season produces, how anything is made or that even food might be connected to living plants and animals. They are not alone in this. The modern mass-produced food industry prides itself on its lack of accountability and identity. If you have the money it will deal its wares to anyone, anywhere, anytime. There is not a smidgeon of honesty, intimacy or responsibility about it.

I realised from the outset that if this scheme were to have maximum effect then it should have minimum impact. It should be as small as possible and infinitely adaptable. In every detail it should respond to local conditions. The offenders should come from the local community. The produce should be dictated entirely by local soil and climate and everything should go back out to that community. People would know who we are and could come and see what we were up to. We would be accountable.

We use as little machinery as possible and are proudly low-tech. Ingenuity and graft counts for much more than the ability to sit on a huge tractor listening to the radio.

We are not interested in growing anything out of season, having an early or late supply or competing in any way with the weather. We cheat nobody, least of all ourselves. It is still early days. Our little six-acre plot in Herefordshire has only been up and running since August 2005. But the plan is to create a pilot site that could be replicated anywhere else in the country precisely because no two locations would be alike. Each site would share the same ethos but make it work in its own image.

We grow vegetables that thrive in the micro environment of the land which is heavy, sticky, bloody awkward clay. Our animals are chosen for their meaning and historical relationship to that area. Every possible point of connection should be made if at all possible. We visit local cheese and ice-cream makers, see apples harvested and turned into cider, see sausages made and visit an abattoir. Connections, connections.

It is a tiny group. Sometimes as few as two can come. The most we have ever had on one day is seven. But they actively engage with the pigs, sheep and chickens, they check the garlic to see if it has grown and they brave filthy weather to hand dig land drains, or do an awkward piece of fencing. It has become personal.

I want my group to learn to respect the land, animals and crops. To respect the food and the labour that has produced it and then to share it locally with as many people as possible. If they can do that then there seems to be a real chance that just a few of them might translate that respect first back to themselves and then to their fellow citizens. In the process I hope that I show in this book how we can save the taxpayer millions – if not billions. But the balance sheet is human as well as fiscal.

What follows was written over the year, often late at night when dog-tired or very early in the mornings and always on top of doing a full day's work. All speech was recorded the same day from memory or scribbled notes and I believe I have been true to words and events. It is an entirely personal story of my relationship with a small group of young people in the middle of the countryside in provincial England. 'Gardeners' World' it is not.

Beginning: First of November 2005

Beginning: First of November 2005
Not spring. Not spring at all

Very, very tired. And, as ever, when tired I get completely uninterested in most things. The project feels like endless hassle. Either everyone is humouring me or else they really think that I know what I am doing. I don't.

Got back from book talk at the Crucible Theatre in Sheffield just after midnight, chauffeur-driven big car, full theatre, applause, autographs, blah blah. As ever I felt an impostor until I got on stage. Then the logic of performance and tightrope walking takes over. Keep going and don't look down. A few hours sleep then up and into work clothes and the Land Rover with the floor a deep litter of crisps packets and the tailgate held up with bailer twine.

It was a lovely autumnal morning with thin sun floating to the ground through yellowing leaves, but the day was bleak.

Only three came, Andrés, Deaf Andy and Kate. Kate was obviously in a bad way – going through 'the rattle' as she describes withdrawal. Her methadone prescription that she gets as a heroin substitute – which they invariably refer to as their 'script' – had been reduced from 40 mls to 20 (although that jump is unlikely). She was sweating, shivering and her nose streamed. In the afternoon she was sick – openly, with projection and in front of us all – about four or five times.

She showed me her diary which was intense, schoolgirlish, articulate and beautifully written. Her self-loathing is overwhelming as is her hatred for her addiction. She has used crack and heroin over the weekend having tried to avoid it but failed.

19

This means that she has failed her drug testing. The reduction in methadone means that she is cold turkeying from that and craving heroin as the much more accessible solution. If she were not at the farm she would do anything (although she claims short of prostitution or mugging) to get that 'bag'. They all talk of £10 bags as their standard currency.

We moved the pigs, moved the pigs' ark (the movable housing with a rounded corrugated iron roof), tidied up and put down new bedding – and spent a lot of time playing with pigs.

Andrés told me that I was saving his life.

We turned the compost heap and marked out beds in the polytunnel. I showed them how to dig. We walked the fences and discussed our fencing policy and how best to tackle the pond. But all this was overshadowed by Katie's misery.

As ever we talked over lunch (which was good – people ate without too many fights and only Deaf Andy refused to touch what was offered; Rocky persuaded him to eat a bacon roll however). Kate told us that her mother had left when she was a few months old, leaving her father with four children. All were taken into care. She was taken back to her father when she was seven, sobbing at being removed from her (foster) mummy. Her two older brothers and sisters were left in care. She met her mother again when she was fourteen. She lives in Walsall with her 'paki boyfriend' ('I mustn't say that. He's Indian really. He's a good bloke really.') When she first went there, Kate saw her mother's boyfriend borrow ten quid to go up the road. Kate thought he was off to buy drugs. No, her mother said, he's just off to see the girls up the road.

All afternoon she was on the phone trying to get her dad to give her the digibox so she could sell it to buy a bag. She said that she might try and get back to prison so that she could stop using. As long as she is with people who have crack and heroin around not using is impossibly difficult.

She left with us all knowing she would almost certainly use tonight.

20

Deaf Andy says that he only uses 'at night. Occasionally'. Occasionally turns out to mean about five times a week. He is also on a script of 90 ml of methadone. He says that he has used almost daily for eleven years.

I love that bag more than anything in this world. It's the devil. I hate it.

He lives in a car parked outside his mother's house. He says it's all right until you go into the warmth of a house. Then it's horrible going back outside. At this Andrés murmurs, You get used to it. He means living in a cardboard box.

I ask Deaf Andy why he lives in the car. The court put an order on him not allowing him into his house.

It would have been OK if I hadn't beat up my stepdad.

Oh yeah? Why?

I took twelve pills and had an argument with him

We ask for a bit more info.

He said I was wrong and I wasn't so I lashed into him. It was only because of the pills though. I felt like Mr Concrete. Twelve Mitsubishis. You see I took about five then took some more to see if they were working. Then I forgot how many I had taken. But I reached eleven so I rounded it up to the dozen. And some coke. I felt like . . . like . . . what's the word? Like concrete.

He is very thin. Goes to the gym most days. But I gives up. Me arms hurt.

It is hard to feel sorry for him. He is petulant and spoilt. He was born profoundly deaf but had an operation and got some hearing. He has a speech defect and I suspect has been spoilt by his mother and Nan. To me he seems lost but is surprisingly strong and independent. But I can't see how it can go anywhere good.

Andrés is busy and friendly all day. He is very quick and funny. Looks healthier by the day. He is on 70 mls of methadone and is always the most vehement to speak against heroin. He has lived on the streets and now lives in a hostel. Is thirty-one. Is

21

stick-thin and cowed. Looks beaten. Is sick of it. His teeth are rotting. Just getting some life back into him seems like a triumph. Then today he quietly said that he had spent his money (what money? The Dole I suppose) on clothes on Friday. On Saturday he sold them all for a bag or two. He is using 'just once a week or so'.

They all lie. It is probably much more. I want to be worldly and cynical. But I want to believe all the good.

They told me that Wayne was sent to prison yesterday for stealing diesel from a truck. He can't drive. Apparently he has smuggled in a bag with him. Kate said this means he won't be rattling until this afternoon. But prison will let him withdraw and get his embolism seen to. He will come out and start using straight away – perhaps in as little as four weeks (he got four months).

God God God.

Their lives are such a spiral of disaster and loss.

Someone said to me today, I hope that you are writing all this down. I'm not. So much has happened but I'm usually too exhausted to attempt to record it but I must try. The family complain that I bring it all home, talk about nothing else. Maybe writing it down more would exorcise it. Maybe I would sleep.

Spring 2005

Let's go back a year.

In the months before Christmas 2004 I visited a whole range of muddy fields on grey midwinter afternoons. Herefordshire is one of the most beautiful, unspoilt counties in Britain but the countryside in winter is usually a dirty, stinking, cold, very brown place. The encircling grey of a Northern European autumn used to be relieved by stubble. The cornfields were cleared of their harvest and the ensuing bales were brought in under cover to provide bedding for the winter cattle and then gradually the fields were ploughed ready for the next seed to be sown. This process happened ritualistically over the course of the winter and as long as the work was done by springtime when the ground warmed up so that sown seed would germinate then there was no haste involved. The weather worked at the soil on heavy land, breaking it down, but on the chalk downs where I was raised sometimes the stubble remained right through to March or even April. This reflected a tawny light back from the ground. Early autumn stubble fields were hard and scratchy on bare legs and then gradually became softer and muddier as winter progressed. But there was an accessibility about them. Locals walked their dogs and got to know the land. Farmers recognised the silhouettes of the dogs and their walkers. Small connections were made and there was a sense of poise between two acts, that balanced the year. Now tractors are so powerful that they can rip through the land at any time of year and wheat is almost invariably sown as soon as the previous crop is lifted. The landscape shifts overnight from the gold of harvest to dirty brown. A season has been ruthlessly ploughed into the ground and the fields are locked rooms.

But it was a good time to be looking. Anywhere looks attractive in the full pomp of May or June. If you want to know the true face of a piece of land it is probably best to see its closed, brown winter face.

I was looking for a few fields to rent near enough to me so that I could engage with it on a daily basis – certainly no more than thirty minutes by winding road and ideally near enough to pop over to open a greenhouse or feed the pigs if need be. One site seemed perfect and negotiations went well until the owner suddenly put his farm up for sale.

Then we found another farm about twenty minutes west of Leominster. The owners were ideal – thoughtful, wise people, farming organically, building an eco-house and profoundly interested in the subject. But the site felt wrong. With hindsight I now believe it could have worked well but I had inarticulate, visceral reservations and there were complications with access and usage that would only get worse. Also there was an existing group that I was very keen to work with over the coming year that was based in Worcester, which was local in the context of the UK or even the region, but it was that extra twenty minutes west that was the spoiler. It added another chunk of car-cramped time to what was already over an hour on country roads after the last person had been collected. It was a little too far for that group. To put together a more local group would have meant tedious bureaucracy across Hereford, Ludlow and Welsh probation offices and have delayed the project with probable knock-on effects on the growing season. All my working life I had run my own business or been self-employed. If I wanted things to happen I did it. If I could not do it I asked someone else to do it for me. That was it. But now, for the first time in my life, I was dealing with bureaucracy and institutions. Even the simplest thing seemed to become mysteriously complicated and happen at a snail's pace. So, along with my rumbling misgivings about the site itself, I was loath to add a layer of complication with that extra twenty minutes and we prevaricated.

Then, out of nowhere, we were offered a site in a village called Monkland literally across the fields from my house. I can see it now as I write these words. It was a long thin field of a couple of acres and a scrap of ground next to it that had been used for storing agricultural machinery. Another block of land came with it about half a mile away, which we could defer for a year. After months of searching this place appeared under my nose. It was almost too good to be true.

Negotiations were entered into and, predictably, they ground exceedingly slow. I started looking around for tools, greenhouses, buildings, perhaps a second-hand tent to provide short-term shelter, a field kitchen, compostable toilets, fencing – you know, all the little things that make a smallholding conform to all the health and safety regulations possible. I pricked out hundreds of tomato plants, sowed courgettes, pumpkins and celeriac ready for planting out after the last frosts. My greenhouse and cold frames began to overflow.

An advert was put in the *Hereford Times* for a manager. Due to the mechanics of government recruiting, a full three weeks was given before any response was made to the telephone responses and then each applicant was sent a long form to fill out. Remember this is Herefordshire and the local paper. If you want a job, a Jack Russell puppy, a used pushchair or a car you look in the paper and ring the number on the ad. Perhaps you go and see them. The deal is lost or done the same day. But eventually I got a phone call from the probation service at Hereford to ask me to come in for a meeting to draw up the shortlist. Despite my chronic aversion to meetings – based on the fact that they interrupt 'real' work to get so very little actually done – I went along. We discussed the first two applicants – both OK – when it was announced that that was it. There were only two applicants who had returned the complex and exceedingly dreary forms that they had to fill in.

✻   ✻   ✻

Manager required for a new organic smallholding near Leominster

This is an exciting new project training unemployed men and women from a range of backgrounds in agricultural and horticultural skills. This will include vegetable, herb and fruit production as well as animal husbandry. Whilst the project is intended primarily to provide training opportunities, it will also operate commercially.

The job will involve setting up and ensuring the smooth running of the project. We are looking for an individual with an organic and/or biodynamic farming or horticulture background who also has project management skills and the ability to work well with people.

The successful applicant would be expected to take responsibility for managing all aspects of the smallholding although experts in various disciplines will visit when required.

The contract is for two years in the first instance with a permanent post depending on the success of the project.

Closing date 28th April

Salary 16–19k p.a. depending on experience.

✻   ✻   ✻

When it finally came round to interviewing them only one of them turned up. His name was Philip Lloyd and he appeared to be well equipped to do the job, was the contractor already working the farm that the site was on so knew it well and seemed to be genuinely interested in the project and its goals. He also seemed to be a decent man. Despite the lack of any choice, rather than go through the interminable procedure of re-advertising, he was offered the job. I was happy with this. If the only applicant was good enough then one was all you needed.

So things were shaping up. Later than we expected or wanted, we had a site, a manager and more offenders than we could shake a stick at. We were ready to get going. Or so I naively thought.

Later that day a visit to the site was organised for offenders who might be using it. Two groups, one from Hereford and another from Worcester. Only one of the Hereford bunch, a girl of twenty-five, turned up. Not turning up is apparently a predictable pattern, especially when it will lead to more trouble than it is worth.

But the Worcester lot were all there and all pretty much dressed alike in white trainers, white jeans and baseball caps with plenty of bling and tattoos. They hardly fitted the agricultural image. All were unnaturally pale, fidgety and had bad skin. Chuck in a hoodie or two and they would complete the alienated, scary stereotype but they seemed to me to be more like overgrown school kids on a field trip. I shook their hands and tried to remember each name. One, called Martin, was a large bloke in a Burberry baseball cap; he pushed himself forward and spoke a lot, dominant but friendly. Another, called Wayne, was small, with dark hair and a huge smile that he only broke to lick his lips. I didn't know then that heroin and methadone give you a permanently dry mouth. I caught a Lee but never worked out which of the two hiding at the back, saying nothing, he was. One called Adam with curiously yellow skin and a worried expression was easy to remember because he had the same name as my son. His voice was more articulate and confident than the others. They all spoke with a distinct accent – to my ears an attractive mixture of rural Worcestershire and West Midlands twang.

Most were clutching cans of Coke and I told them that this was the last time any fizzy drink or junk food would appear on site. We would eat what we were trying to grow and rear to sell to other people. Proper food but plenty of it. They grinned or nodded in what I then thought was disdain or acceptance of that concept but I now, a year down the road, know was incredulity. They hadn't a clue as to what I was talking about. I was also blissfully ignorant of the battles that lay ahead in getting them to accept and eat what I blithely called 'proper food' although one probation officer had already told me that the most important thing that I could do for most of them when they turned up to work would be to give them breakfast as you could guarantee that none would have had any.

I piled all eight into my Land Rover and drove them over the road to the second part of the site, twenty odd acres set back off the road. Real fields. I now know that they would have seen that as a haven, a chance for safe retreat. At the time I was perhaps a little over-eager to stress how productive it could become through their engagement and hard work. But they liked bumping around in the Land Rover.

They were interested, surprisingly knowledgeable about growing things and raising animals and keen to start, preferably that instant. Could we pull the docks, cut down trees, drive a tractor? Reining them in a little, we made a date for the next week. I suggested an 8 a.m. start and was met with blank disbelief. In fact it turned out to be completely impractical because most of them had to collect their 'scripts' of methadone from the chemists, which didn't open until nine. The earliest they could get to me would be 10.30 a.m. Hardly up with the lark but then the lark wasn't a user trying to straighten themselves out. They would be brought over by Rocky, their ex-policeman driver, minder and an endlessly patient and wise guardian.

The following week we had been invited to visit the parish council to chat about the project. There was no permission to be asked for as we were not proposing anything illegal or that needed planning consent. If the offenders were not working on the smallholding they would otherwise have been doing some kind of work for and in the community, fixing footpath signs, painting bus shelters or cleaning chewing gum off the streets somewhere else in the region. I understood this meeting to be in the form of a presentation to the parish council members to explain what we were doing and, most importantly, to ask them for help and cooperation in any way that they felt was suitable or possible. It was an opportunity to explain and celebrate the start of something exciting.

I went over there at about eight o'clock on one of those May evenings when the countryside is almost fluorescent with cow parsley, May blossom and a fierce intensity of green. Nowhere, no how could ever be more beautiful and I endure many bleak days of the year for just a few hours like this. But when I arrived at the village hall everyone looked rather grim. There were also many more people than could possibly constitute a parish council. It turned out that this was both the AGM and a council meeting and that a flyer had been circulated warning people of the horrors of 'criminals' secretly being infiltrated into the village, living in a tented town on site and perfectly poised to rob everyone and everything.

The quiet chat with an admiring local council turned out to be a million miles from what followed. David Chantler, the chief probation officer, and I, spent the best part of an hour facing what appeared to be a mob of angry villagers expressing extreme hostility. It was a shocking and deeply unpleasant turn of events. There was some support, but this was muted and took much courage in the teeth of aggressive hostility. Most of the worries were entirely unfounded (such as a rumour that we were building a young offenders' prison on this site) and we explained that 6–12 young people, all over eighteen, always accompanied by an ex-policeman and a community worker (which incidentally would make it the best policed community in the whole of Hereford-shire) would come and work on the smallholding 2–3 days a week for six hours and then go home. All lived in the community

31

and none were being punished for a crime that otherwise warranted a custodial sentence. We were not 'bringing in' dangerous criminals but providing an opportunity for people who would anyway be legitimately out and about in the community and who were perfectly at liberty to visit the village at any time of day or night. They were, and this was a refrain I was to hear myself repeat on TV, radio and in the press, our neighbours or families. They were us.

We explained that we did not want to impose anything without their blessing because the entire scheme was based upon integrating people into communal life. The intention was to give something back to the rural community and do something positive for our young people. The project could be adapted and to an extent supervised by a local steering body. It could be made very small and would never grow because if it was a huge success then it would be replicated elsewhere rather than increase in size.

None of this cut much ice. The objections were many but a few cropped up again and again:

Who will chase after them when they run away across the fields?

Who will compensate us when we are robbed or worse?

How do we know that they will not be casing all the houses locally and then come back with their friends months later and pillage them?

Why spend money on 'bad' people when there are good people who need money?

Who will compensate us for the lowering of our house prices?

Why here?

Why us?

It was clear that they were frightened of an unknown that they saw as being brought in from 'away' to potentially defile their lives. It is not an unreasonable fear. I am a fan of NIMBYism insofar that our backyards are the place where we live. If we don't care for them then no one will. But I tried to point out that this was my backyard too. My children had grown up there, been to school with their children. If anyone was going to suffer it was likely to be me and my family. I was quickly corrected on this. I lived more than a mile away, in another parish. I was as foreign as rampaging, pillaging junkies were.

We got nowhere. Some people were brave enough to stand up and proclaim their support but the loudest were violently – and even though I do not shy from confrontation, it did feel astonishingly hostile and violent – opposed to it. I stressed that it could only work if we had their cooperation, albeit it was entirely unnecessary in terms of planning or legality. Half the audience wanted a vote there and then but it was decided that the matter should be put to the vote via the electoral roll after a week's deliberation. They would inform us of the result as soon as it was known.

It was not all despair. As the meeting broke up a surprising number came up to me and wished me well with the project and apologised for the hostility shown. It did not seem impossible that that mood of acceptance might grow as people thought it through.

One of the ironies of this was that a mile or two away a local farmer had established a camp of over two thousand fruit pickers from Eastern Europe to service the hundreds of acres of poly-tunnels he had erected over the winter that had openly flouted all planning laws and public opposition, yet was allowed to do this without any let or hindrance. Our tiny group of half a dozen or so local people that would almost be outnumbered by supervisors and only present for a maximum of twenty hours a week were seen as a far greater threat.

*　　*　　*

A few days later I met the group and Rocky in a café on the Malvern Hills. There was Adam, two brothers – Lee and Paul – Wayne with the huge grin looking about twelve, Martin – the big lumbering bear of a man who had dominated our last meeting at Monkland – and another lad called Tom with a broad Northern Irish accent and a wriggly inability to stay still. Again, I was struck, in mid and radiant June, by the waxy pallor of their faces.

I told them of the reaction at the meeting and that people thought of them as monsters of depravity and crimes on legs. They were disappointed and dismayed but not really outraged. Perhaps they were used to this kind of rejection.

I told them that I was not going to give up. We would find another site and we would show all the people that we could do it well. A lot of people considered them a useless, dangerous bunch of junkies who should be locked up and the key thrown away. It was up to us to show these people that they were wrong.

Inevitably I talked at them, which was the last thing that I wanted to do. I needed to spend time with them, to work side by side and chat rather than being the bloke off the telly making pronouncements and promises. I realised that I knew nothing about them. Nothing about their lives at all. I had no briefing about them in any way. We were in this together but hardly knew each other's names. But we got a cup of tea and the talk became smaller, less structured.

Adam Harrison, the most articulate of the group, said: The truth is I'm sick of it Monty. I've had enough of it. I'm twenty-seven and it's time I grew up, got a job, got a girlfriend. Somewhere to live. I've been using for nearly fifteen years. I'm sick and tired of it.

Fifteen years? You must have been twelve?

Twelve, thirteen. Around then. I remember injecting into my groin in the school toilets so the teachers wouldn't see the marks when we did PE and I had to wear shorts. It's not good Mont. It can't go on.

A couple of days later the ballot was held and, whilst I was filming for 'Gardeners' World', I heard that they had decided not to welcome the project by a vote of 98 to 36. This was an overwhelming vote against with a turnout of over 80 per cent.

I got a call from my two youngest children who were alone in the house to say that two men, one with a great lens on his camera, were taking pictures through the windows of my house, snooping around my garden and giving my fourteen-year-old son the fourth degree as to my whereabouts. Sixty miles away, my mobile phone was in a state of permanent buzz from other members of the press wanting to speak to me. My agent and office at home were both fending off another batch of enquiries. Whilst this may be an average day for a film or football star, I assure you that this is not normal for a plodding TV gardener.

I met the group to tell them of the vote (despite the fact that it had been plastered all over radio, TV and newspapers) at a local farm that had a project designed to introduce animals and vegetables for handicapped children.

Martin, the big lad who had been so buoyant a week earlier sat catatonically away from the group, white trousers and Burberry baseball cap slightly askew. His mouth hung open and his eyes were glazed.

What's up? I asked.

Rocky caught my eye and quietly said, He's OK. Although he was clearly anything but OK I demurred, instantly out of my depth. The others took no notice of him at all. The place was inspiring but also a reproach. It made only too clear what we had failed to set up. There were vegetables growing in raised beds, pigs, ducks, chickens, lambs and calves in a field. Although rather neater and voyeuristic than anything I had envisaged it would have been ideal for us. They all took pictures of each other on their phones with the largest of the pigs and tiptoed fastidiously around the mud and poo.

I also told them about the dozens of letters and emails I had received supporting the project and offering sites around the country. They just had to hang on for a little longer whilst we found a site.

Later that week they came to see me at the big 'Gardeners' World Live' show at the NEC in Birmingham. I felt flattered. On one level I am sure that none of them would ever have attended that kind of show without the official structure of the project but it began to feel as though we were in something together. Martin was alert and engaged again. At one point I noticed him gently usher a young child through the encircling crowd to get an autograph. It was a small act of private kindness and considera- tion. I wondered what the villagers who had voted to exclude him from the parish boundary would have thought.

Over the next few weeks we had a couple of meetings with the parish council to see what could be salvaged from the situation. They were uniformly apologetic, generous and supportive. But I knew that we would have to abandon the site even though we had committed ourselves to a two-year lease. The figures from the vote could not be ignored. To push on against prevailing local goodwill would have been against the entire ethos of the project. Once the dust had settled it seemed that the greatest grievance was the lack of communication rather than the notion that criminals might be in their midst. We – the probation service, BBC (the fact that it was being filmed was a huge black mark for most villagers) and not least poncy, overpaid TV gardener – were thinking we could do just what we liked without the decency to at least discuss it with the community first. In all our high- minded fervour we had overlooked simple good manners.

The result was that after six months' work, hiring a manager, organising a group and committing ourselves to two years' rental of 20-odd acres of land, we had no site. All dressed up and nowhere to go. If it had been November or January it would have been embarrassing and difficult but as it was late May and every day was, in growing terms, a day lost, it was, by any measure, an unmitigated disaster.

However, I tried to analyse what we needed to bear in mind for the future so at least the fiasco could have some positive use. These are the notes I made at the time:

- We should have contacted the parish council as soon as we even thought of using the site. Without that formal level of blessing the scheme cannot be accepted by a local rural community.
- We hugely underestimated the power and speed of rumour. At this type of location every unknown car, every strange face, is noted and remarked upon. Local people knew about the site as a proposed location within days if not hours of the very first prospective visit. It was extremely naive to think that we could treat the site as insulated from the community until such a time as we chose to integrate it. The rumours that spread were wildly inaccurate – an open prison, a tented village, paedophiles, rapists etc. – but mud had stuck by the time we were in a position to try and set the record straight.
- We should have very clearly explained the details of the project and requested the community's cooperation in making it a success before we even committed ourselves to the tenancy. In practice this was not needed and almost certainly would not be forthcoming, but the process of being seen to request acceptance is very important.
- We were cavalier with details on the basis that the essence of the scheme was more important. To village people, any slight change in the acreage of the project was seen as an example of our deviousness and duplicity. These things matter.
- There was a lack of cohesive organisation – and to a degree this remains. The nature of this project means that things slip into the void between the probation service, the Trust, the BBC and my own office. I strongly believe that it needed – and

any future sites will need – a central individual with sole responsibility for setting up and managing the sites, the relationships with the local communities and the public at large. This would not include any of the day-to-day details of the sites but would act as the hub at the centre of the wheel. No one individual was – or is – responsible for this work. As a result contacts were not made, letters not written and even within the project, details not shared. This was a role that would ideally suit a young, enthusiastic person, ideologically engaged with the project who has the time, ability and resources to act efficiently and fast. Too often we – and I include myself in this criticism – reacted slowly and ineptly.

- It was a mistake to offer them a vote or to agree to abide by the result of a vote. This was a cul-de-sac that gave us no room to manoeuvre and I take much of the responsibility for that. The local community has to be engaged from the outset, informed and allowed to present their views – but we must always retain our rights to make our own decisions.

- We underestimated the extent of press interest. Although this elicited much national sympathy and interest, this will always play badly with a rural community. Those against the scheme knew that they would look bad – and this only aggravated their opposition.

On the longest day – literally the highlight of my year – I went and spoke to the West Mercia Probation Area Staff Conference at Ludlow racecourse. It was called – rather ominously – 'Implement, Innovate, Integrate'. I was specifically under the 'Innovate' heading.

As my contribution to innovation I talked about the fiasco of Monkland but enthused as best I could for the hopes of a more successful future. I didn't have to make that up. I knew it could work – just didn't know how, where, when or with whom. It was a good job they hadn't put me under the 'Integrate' section.

One of the good things to come out of the resulting national publicity was the immediate offer of dozens of alternative sites, some of which were local and more convenient for Rocky's group.

I visited several locally, all of which were good but all with a few problems, not least neighbours and communities which now loomed in our minds as a far bigger hurdle than matters agricultural.

One letter in particular came from David and Tricia Reeve, owners of a farmhouse and patch of land called, reassuringly, 'The Rock' which was halfway between Leominster and Tenbury Wells and twenty minutes from Ludlow. Although still not exactly local to the group's starting point in Worcester (in fact they were more far-flung than that and collecting them involved up to an hour's trawl around the countryside stopping off to pick them up) it was no further than Monkland had been.

Despite its relative proximity to three market towns it is set in one of the remotest, most 'lost' pieces of countryside remaining in Britain in the twenty-first century. It is one of those places that can be arrived at from a dozen different roads, all twisting and winding between tall hedges and all swallowing up car and driver with laughable ease. In the months that followed I would dread the words 'sat nav' when it came to giving instructions for deliveries. Satellite navigation might be great for towns (I have never used one) but it has never yet managed to deliver anyone accurately to the Rock.

I went along at the end of June to have a look. It immediately felt good but then it was midsummer and the English countryside had its best face on. I tried to look at it with an objective eye. The facts were bald and brief. It was almost comically remote, had six acres of paddock, some adjacent buildings including a shed that could be converted into a mess hut, a couple of concrete yards for dry standing and extremely decent and well-intentioned prospective landlords.

It felt workmanlike. The one field ran in a slope down to a boundary made up of huge oaks and ashes – presumably an overgrown hedge. The result was that it concealed both view in and out. From one of the oaks a buzzard heaved itself into the air and drifted over us. I rummaged a hand through the grass, scudding the soil at its roots. Clay. The grass had been cut for hay so was short and it felt rather empty in the daunting way that a cleared factory floor can. Farmland only has meaning when it is used and managed. Perhaps that was just a reflection of my anxiety.

At the top of the slope there was a belt of planted woodland which screened off a large turkey unit. We have just such a factory farm next door to us at home and I noticed the familiar sickly smell of the place. Well, that was modern Britain and they were a neighbour. If we took the site we would have to get along. Turning and looking down the hill I saw that on the other two sides were fields in the unstructured mesh of land cleared from woodland rather than enclosed from medieval open fields. We would be completely unoverlooked. To see any of the site you had to be on it. A dried-up pond was down on another corner and a ditch filled with a tangle of brambles and willow flanked one hedge that had potential for clearing. Winter work. The large farmhouse, typically in the old red sandstone of the Marches, looked out over the field and there was a succession of derelict and semi-derelict stone barns that seemed to be used mainly for storage. A couple of angry geese patrolled the yard and there was a chicken run opposite the back door.

We visited a couple of other sites as well but none had more to offer or fewer disadvantages than this one.

A few weeks later we had a meeting in the barn with local people. Some were very hostile, some extremely keen to be involved and most wary. But the ground was broken and the seed sown. We agreed to set up a steering group with the most vociferous opponents of the scheme invited to sit on it. This steering group would consist of about eight people who would meet once a month at the Rock and we would report to them what we had done. They could ask questions and scrutinise our actions and intentions. They could also act as representatives for the wider community to voice any complaints or anxieties. They could keep an eye on us.

I kept in touch with the group through Rocky. Martin was due in court on 12 July for charges of street robbery that had been brought. I knew he was very worried about this and his drug use had increased accordingly – legal and illegal. He was worried and depressed at the prospect of going back to prison, which seemed inevitable. As it happened the case was adjourned because Martin had got his medication wrong and was too confused to follow the court. But things were not looking good for him.

I was away filming and on holiday for thirty-two days out of forty. Everyone else went on holiday except for the group. You don't get holidays when you are on an order. Not a lot happened slowly. Mid-June became mid-August and the growing season was rapidly running out. Effectively we had lost a whole year.

I got Andy Trim, a biodynamic vegetable grower from near Hay-on-Wye to advise on biodynamics and to help me with the commercial side of vegetable production. Andy is a swashbuckling character, a south London ex-fireman whose laid-back scruffy New-Ageness only thinly disguises an extremely resourceful, practical man with a real understanding of the land and how to look after it. He ran an enormously successful biodynamic smallholding called Fern Verrow with his then wife, Jane. I first met him when I went to interview them for the *Observer* about four years ago and was astonished at the quality of their vegetables. I was not at all sure what they were doing when it came to biodynamics but some of it was clearly very right indeed. Biodynamic growing was developed by Rudolf Steiner in the 1920s and has always seemed to me to be a mixture of hippy

41

mumbo-jumbo and deeply intuitive common sense based upon a holistic understanding of growth. Untangling this has always been beyond me but every single grower that I have spoken to that farms biodynamically says that the quality of their crops increased hugely when they changed to biodynamic growing from just plain organic. None know why but all agree on the evidence in front of them.

At the heart of biodynamic growing is the use of special preparations that involve ritual and highly unscientific manufacture – i.e. stuffing cow horns with manure and burying them over winter because horns are considered to be natural receptacles for cosmic forces, or burying oak bark in a stag's skull and so on. I see this as an almost deliberate way of unlocking the self's ability to intuitively tune in to the larger forces around us. Rationality and science is often counter-productive in this way and if, like me, science always seems to be complete mumbo-jumbo anyway, then I have no problem. But I do have reservations that Steiner formalised a rag-bag of ideas and brought them together in a suspiciously cultish fashion and anyway I never feel at all comfortable blindly following prescriptions. However I do believe that it is important to develop one's instincts and to work directly with all the forces of growth and change. So I thought that we should include it in our project – partly, I confess, because I thought it might appeal to the druggy side of their natures. In fact I was wrong about that. It is me that is the child of the sixties.

Anyway Andy came along, challenged all my preconceptions of where to position things and how to set about it and generally inspired enthusiastic thought and confusion.

September 2005

David and Tricia Reeve

David: We came to the Rock in January 1997. We selected this area by looking at a night sat photo because where we were renting was too bright. But the Marches was the nearest to civilisation that was still black. We went up onto the Malverns on a clear night and to the east the sky was awash with yellow sodium lights but to the west, in Herefordshire, it was pitch black.

We were in Zimbabwe from 1989–95, initially in the army and then we stayed on running Operation Raleigh South Africa. I retired in 1992 after thirty-one years in the Worcestershire and Sherwood Foresters. My rank? Major.

We got married in 1959. That's forty-six years now. Tricia is seventy and I was sixty-nine the other day.

We saw the report in the *Hereford Times* about the problems you had at Monkland and we thought what a pity. It seemed to be a scheme that ought to have a chance. We had the same amount of land available so I wrote to you.

Tricia: We were fed up with making hay. It's jolly hard work and for two pounds a bale it just wasn't economical.

David: We did let it a few times. In one case disastrously. Chap didn't pay and had to take him to court. But we got the money.

Tricia: On the internet. Dead easy.

David: We are obviously enthusiastic about the scheme as a matter of principal but in all honesty we had little idea what it would be like. We knew that you wanted some kind of Market Garden set-up. We didn't know about the livestock. But that was no problem. We had no idea about the personalities. In fact we were pleasantly surprised by the people who turned up.

Tricia: Everyone deserves a second chance. To knock them back just because they have committed crimes is just plain unfair. We had worked with youth clubs in the army. If they are not bored then they are contributing but if they are bored then they get into mischief. Raleigh took all sorts and at the end of three months they had gelled and it did them a lot of good.

1/9/05

The lease for the land at the Rock runs for one year from today. It has taken nine months to get this far.

5/9/05

The project team turn up to film me being filmed at BBC's 'Gardener of the Year'. As always when two crews are in each other's space there is a certain amount of wariness and rivalry. The purpose is to show what a busy chap I am. But not busy enough yet to make this thing happen. And in truth I don't feel remotely busy when filming. I am just working like everyone else except my job has lots of breaks and is not very demanding.

7/9/05

First day not filming for 8 days and took it as a day off although I went over to the Rock for a couple of hours for a meeting with Philip – who is now apparently close to agreeing a contract – and Andy Trim. Philip is clearly not convinced about the need for a biodynamic approach and after half an hour says that he thinks biodynamics is crazy and he wants no part in it and storms off. Awkwardness all round. Andy is positive and and helpful and challenges much of what Philip and I had suggested to each other. Later on I see Andy and Philip talking together so presumably they come to some kind of mutual agreement to differ.

Ray Harris, pig expert from Vowchurch, came along to check out the site and advise us as he is giving us four Tamworths. Ray is fanatical about pigs and sees the site (the world?) as a place primarily to be focused around their welfare. I can sustain this for half an hour or so but tire a little beyond that, having exhausted my range of porcine conversation. It is a far cry from the manicured back gardens of 'Gardener of the Year'.

Mostly new faces in the group although the brothers Lee and Paul were there and smiling Wayne. Tall man, Andrés (but perhaps Andy. Both are used) thin as a post and haunted look. Face like a medieval martyr. He said that he was still using as he had no script yet.

He radiates unhappiness.

That evening I google 'Andrés Pope + heroin + Worcester' and get a newspaper report published in January last year (2004).

Andrés is described as being twenty-nine and a heroin user. He apparently stole meat worth £28 and three watches amounting to £100. The watches were recovered and the meat nabbed when he tried to flog them in a pub. The police recovered seventeen packets of meat which means that they must have been less than two pounds

47

each. It is scavenging, scraping around. The DTTO (drugs treatment and testing order) was for six months so would have expired. His presence with us must be as a result of a further crime and order.

There are a range of orders and sub-orders that are geared to trying to deal with specific problems and focus police and probationary resources where they can be most effective. This is clearly laudable and effective but it does translate into yet more layers of bureaucracy all with their own arcane jargon and frenzy of acronyms. So our group are all part of the Prolific and Other Priority Offenders Strategy (PPO) launched in September 2004. The idea is to reduce the offending of 15–20 criminals in each Crime and Disorder Reduction Partnership (CDRP). This amounts to some 8,000 particularly active crims in the UK. Most of these are persistent drug users (PDUs) who commit multiple crimes daily to support their drug habits.

Mind you, as Rocky pointed out, the most persistent offenders are the ones that don't get caught.

The group are working on the shed, putting a concrete floor down, building a front wall and fitting a window and door. David Reeve is very much in charge of operations. There is not a lot else to do yet but they seem to be enjoying it although the ground is hard, we have no tools, no seed and it is the wrong time of year. Tomorrow, when I am filming at GW, they have a first aid session.

They have started a daybook and Rocky is encouraging as many as possible to write something – anything – on each visit. They do this studiously and without self-consciousness. It is a strange document, personal and yet not at all private. The writing is often a scrawl and the spelling erratic at best but it is a powerful and often funny document. Re-reading it, the thing that strikes me most is the discrepancy between my perception of the events, remarks and atmosphere of the day and their recorded comments.

07.09.05

Met Monty for the first time, had chat with him about things. Helped the lad cutting wood for the barn. Sometimes feel paranoid about fitting in and doing the correct thing.

Andy Pope

On the way to Middleton-on-the-Hill, found out my court case is in today's Worcester Evening News. It's front page news and fills it too. I'm not very happy with the situation but have to live with it. People around the City who read it and know me are not going to be happy but what can I do??? I'm very apprehensive about seeing family members too as I'm worried about their response to it . . . The other dwellers around my estate worry me too as I'm worried about their response.

Lee Raymond

Early start today, met Monty – seemed safe. Shed is coming along nicely and will be soon finished. Had a bit of a sandwich and threw it up. Still feeling bad but today is the first day of me being reduced off my Meth.

Chris

08.09.05

Had a good day, glad I came, enjoyed First Aid Course, upset with myself for turning up under the influence. Can't help feeling I've let people down. Sorry, really am sorry.

Andy B

13/9/05

Fine dewy morning. Met Philip at the Rock at 7 a.m. An element of machismo in this. Neither of us admitting that this was unusually early to be doing such things. We talked through sites of ploughed areas and fencing to be done with the layout of the field for veg, animals etc. It feels, inevitably, a bit hypothetical and rushed. Better to muddle and move by instinct in such things, but we don't have that luxury.

19/9/05

Drove over to Llandrindod Wells to talk to Powys council about the project. Massed ranks of social workers, probation officers, police etc., etc. in a horseshoe around the room. I said my bit, stressing the drugs side of things and the problems that we had had setting the site up at Monkland. A hand went up.

Does it have to be hard drugs? Because I don't think that we have enough people for that in Powys.

In practice the hardest thing in a sparsely populated area like Powys is assembling everyone together. The council positive and energetic and I believe that they will set something up.* I came away with a sense of spreading beyond the limitations of the site and all the problems of setting it up.

Marsha, my assistant, has been hard at work trying to source a greenhouse, tractor, seeds, tools, pig arks, hen houses, fencing – all the stuff that one needs to set up a small farm but without any resources – not even human ones because we don't have time. It is all hassle.

---

* In fact I have not heard from them since so it seems to have come to nothing.

20/9/05

The first really big day. We had booked a team of horses and plough with handler to come and turn the first furrow. This was intended as both a symbolically low-tech act and frankly entertainment for the group. With hindsight I should have floated the idea and let them be part of it. I presumed a fascination with the symbolic act of turning the first turf that they just didn't share.

Tom (the talkative, wriggly Northern Irish lad who came to Malvern. I learn that he had apparently watched members of his family executed and had punishment beating/shooting before being kicked out of N. Ireland with his mum at very short notice. Like an hour short). Katie, the only girl; skeletal thin and unhappy but wanting to like the horses. Andrés, Paul, Lee's brother, with a dog. Lee in prison. Chris and lad called Andy (I think) who I did not speak to beyond saying hello.

As it turned out I think I was the most entertained. They seemed largely underwhelmed. This was partly because we had a great crowd of people – most of whom I could not place but seemed to be there in some official capacity – and also a helicopter hired by the BBC to film it all. This rather took the horses' thunder and the group were much more interested in it. They also expressed great resentment that they were not allowed up in it.

However, everybody had a go and ploughed their furrow. It was the first time that I had ploughed with horses and I was surprised by the speed at which they went – you are pulled along in the wake of the earthy wave they make – and the jangly physicality of their presence. There is none of the noisy remoteness of a tractor. It also feels like a big deal – a rite of passage, albeit done at fifty.

We held their attention for about half an hour and then I started wondering what we could actually do. I had banked a lot on the ploughing holding their interest for most of the day. It was exactly the same feeling that I had at the first children's birthday party we held. I worked out a mass of games and had used them all up after twenty minutes. Back then tea and fighting came to the rescue. But neither seemed quite appropriate in this situation.

We have problems about food. Tricia is cooking for them but they reject most of it and seem to be stopping on the way over for some kind of fast junk. This is upsetting Tricia and against the ethos of the whole thing. I will have to talk to Rocky and try and work out a system whereby we all share the same stuff and that's it.

I give them a lecture about not bringing in any food or drink.

That's well out of order Chris says.

Tough. That's the deal.

I'm not coming then. You can't make me go without drink.

It's not fucking prison Kate said.

The BBC crew tell me later that Chris pulled out a bottle of Coke from an inside pocket and told them that he was going to drink it *all* just to show me.

As I talk to them they are almost incapable of concentration and fiddle with their mobile phones or wander about. Feel like banging their heads together.

20.09.05

Today I'm having a real bad day today. DEPRESSED and physically and psychologically and emotionally stressed. Not cause of the team or others around me. I cannot explain where or what has caused it so please be a bit patient with me if I am a little argumentative.

Katie Hirschfield

Big day today. Chopper, Shire horses and the BBC. Monty is here and is supposed to be here all day. I had plough with the horses and found that a good experience. I hope I can do some proper hard work cos hanging around doing nothing is boring me. Even though I'm learning new things I'd rather be doing stuff hands on stuff but altogether it's a good day. No-one's stressed and all is good.

Chris

Not a bad day but more arguing. When will it ever stop. Ha ha. I enjoyed today very much indeed.

Andy B

21/9/05

I got this handwritten report from Andy Trim:

To put together a timed table for the land preparation, and crops etc. I could also prepare a bed layout and cropping plan.

I do some communication by tape, I can record as I think through the work. You can then listen to it at your leisure and it saves me a lot of time, as getting things down on paper is a slow process.

As I have always farmed on a budget, I can obtain most hand tools second hand and reasonably priced from 'Tools for Self Reliance', they are good quality and wooden handled and quality steel.

Regarding larger tractor tools, I have everything necessary to set up.

Ray Harris's son Alan keeps and works ferrets which will be good to get rid of the rabbits.

The organic cow muck, you will need about 50 tons.

Re: Over Wintering Crops
Garlic Variety: Thermadrome – Autumn / Early Winter
                Printadore – Winter/ Early Spring
    Approx 10 Cloves Per Bulb
    Plant 6 inch In The Row 2 Rows To The Bed @ 18
      Inch Broad Beans:
    Super Aquadulce Are Best For Over Wintering
    Each Bean Weighs One Gram – 1000 To The Kilo
    12 Beans To 1
    24 For Double Row @ 18 Inch
    30' Bed Would Require Three Quarters Of A Kilo
    You Could Also Plant Peas (Feltham First),
    Spinach(Giant Winter),
    Propagate Indoors Spring Onions (Offenham
Compacta)
    And Spring Onions.

MOST IMPORTANTLY GET THE GROUND
READY!!!!!

Seed Suppliers:
Edwin Tucker: 01364–652233
Stormy Hall Biodynamic Seed: 01287–661–368
Kings: 01376–570–000

The West Mercia Care Trust – the body that is helping finance
and coordinate the project and whose support is essential to
coordinate and sustain it – is due to meet but I have neither time
nor, in truth, inclination to go to Worcester and sit through a
three-hour meeting. So I email my apologies and write a report to
them on the project to date. It formalises – and dehumanises –
the past few months into a statement. I suppose that this is the
process that follows everyone on both sides of the fence of the
judicial system. It is a world away from any kind of experience in

my working life where I have striven for subjectivity and tying down the emotional or even spiritual response to events as being more permanent and ultimately important than the factual. But I give it a go trying to play the responsible grown-up committee member:

M D NOTES for Trust Meeting 26 September 2005
The best news is that we have started work at the Rock. On 20 Sept we ploughed the first furrow using a beautiful pair of shire horses pulling a single furrow hand plough. Four members of the group were able and willing to take a turn and so be part of what was a hugely significant occasion.

Fifty tons of best cattle manure has been ordered and will be spread and worked in to the ground over the coming week so that raised beds can be made and the first planting – garlic and broad beans – can be made in October.

The team have also done a great deal of work over the past month, guided by David Reeve and Rocky, to build and fit out their own mess room, converting an old woodshed for this purpose. They now consider this space to be their own and are therefore highly motivated to improve and care for it. I have bought crockery, cutlery and simple cooking equipment and Tricia Reeve has been preparing simple lunches for them. This will be supplemented with fresh bread, cheese, fruit and pies that I will buy when I am with them.

Four organically reared weaner piglets have been gifted and will arrive as soon as we have suitable fencing and accommodation and we will purchase sheep in the wake of the fencing. I am buying some pedigree Hereford calves which I will lend to the project for the next year. We shall be making a buying trip to Hereford market to buy hens in the near future.

Finances

There is still a financial void at the centre of the project with little or no financial management or budget. This is a serious flaw and has to be urgently addressed. To date Marsha – who is yet to receive a payment for her work despite being the overwhelmingly important cog in the machine – or myself, my wife or David and Tricia Reeve have been picking up all the bills.

Management

The management and organisation of the day-to-day running remains the problem with the project that really has to be addressed by the Trust if it has any chance of success or even continuation. The probation service is making a first class job of providing and caring for the offenders, liaising with the courts and in that role is at the very hub of the project. It is vital that we retain their enthusiastic support and specialised skills.

My office could run the non-probationary aspect but at the moment does not have the resources, manpower or authority from the Trust. The only solution is to have an individual whose sole job is to run every aspect of the project and to liaise with the various parties concerned. I see no reason why the same individual could not run a series of sites around the Trust's area simultaneously.

The probation service probably could do it although is not doing so at the moment and it would depend upon the suitable individual with boundless enthusiasm, good management skills and sufficient resources to act quickly and efficiently.

At the moment there is a total dislocation of money, authority and action. The only person who is cutting through the various knots to make things happen is Marsha Arnold who is nominally employed one day a week. In practice she spends two or three days a week on the project, subsidised by myself and using the resources of my office. I am happy to provide this but not in an unofficial, ad hoc way. It needs formalising and resolving – soon.

This project is working. It will achieve great things but it will take time, energy and detailed organisation. It will not just happen by default.

27/9/05

A beautiful late summer day. A blue, crystalline sky made busy by swallows gathering fuel for the long journey home (do Africans feel that swallows come 'home' between October and March or that they are visiting? Maybe to a swallow air is home and all points of call just resting places). My journey from home to the Rock through the Herefordshire lanes is a rural road movie, an unholy cross between 'Miss Marple' and 'Scum' and I do it with wonder and dread. When I go and film 'Gardeners' World' I know what I am doing and feel wholly confident that I can cope with any probable eventuality. But every time I set off down these back roads it feels like a bungee jump.

Philip had mown the unploughed grass of the area to be eventually cultivated, marking it out, focusing attention.

Tom, Kate, Andrés, Andy B, Wayne, Paul and Chris arrive about half ten. They stagger out of the car, stiff, carsick, bored and drugged with methadone. It does not exactly constitute a slick, eager workforce. Martin, who has just come out from being on remand, is feeling low and hasn't got his act together to come.

We have a cup of tea, chat a little and then I set the group raking the mown grass, partly so that we can compost it and partly to clear the ground before it is ploughed.

The piece ploughed by the horses is crisp, brown corduroy against the surrounding bleached grass. To me it is lovely land art, worth doing just for the mark on the ground but I think if I were to say such a thing I would be met with derision (we have enough familiarity now to show contempt as and when it pops up) so I hold my pretentiousness to myself. I try to set an example with the raking – hot work in the sun – but most were eager for twenty minutes then fell by the wayside, sloping off for drinks and general collapse. I think that much of this is sheer physical unfitness. They are wrecks, convalescents, just not up to much.

Tom drove David's Land Rover hitched to a trailer and sat watching whilst we loaded and unloaded. He is loud and aggressive in manner yet very likeable. At least, in a slightly zany way, he engages with what we are doing. But he is clearly deeply troubled. He finds David's military bearing and authority a challenge and rears up at any instruction. David is sweetly patient with him.

Paul – 'Razor' – was there with his dog although his brother Lee is now in prison. He says he wants to get clean now – that seeing how his mother reacted to Lee and the grief it is causing her was motivation enough. After lunch he was a lot less engaged and seemed to lose interest in the whole thing.

Lunch is a battlefield. Tom refusing to eat in the same room as anyone else, Kate throwing up and being disgusted by any deviation from what she expected, Andrés sitting facing the wall – no one sitting at the table and joining in. Meals either disturb them or are a symbol of authority that they hate.

Lunch is followed by another twenty-minute spell, then more drinks and smokes and then into the cars for home. In the end I suppose we achieved all of one hour's work.

But it was us, on site, doing something. It was a step forward.

27.09.05

Today we had to rake all the grass up in the field. Monty and David both let me drive the Jeep. Today is one of the days I can also say I have enjoyed myself. Everyday I spend out here with

Monty, I learn something new. I can't wait to start doing the planting so I could learn more about plants and trees. We are also going to clean the pond for some ducks.

Thomas Allen

It is now the end of the day and I can't wait to get home for a bath and a sleep and a fat pipe of weed and a spliff because I feel like I'm starting to get a bit stressed but I must say I quite enjoyed my day at the farm.

Andy B

Have tried to work hard today and have started to rake up grass ready for the compost.

Andy Pope

Good day. Raked field, enjoyed it but pissed off with Rocky following me but never mind, I'll get over it. Everyone got on better!! Enjoyed the day with Monty.

Razor (Paul)

Marsha continued to do a huge amount of work behind the scenes for the project. Amongst the endless organisation of people, places and materials to be done she found time to type up Andy Trim's handwritten notes and send them to me (one room away from where she typed it) as an email. It amounts to a complete analysis and plan of action for the plot.

Date: Tuesday, September 27, 2005 12:07
Subject: Andy's Timetable
What you currently have is an ex arable field that on its recent working life will have been subject to deep ploughing, mechanical cultivation to break up the soil

59

when too wet and too dry and repeated applications of fertilisers and pesticides.

This is shown by the state of the soil and the state of the grass crop currently on it. If you need to verify this send a soil sample to the ADAS (*Adas was founded in 1971 'to provide scientific, technical and business management advice to the agricultural and horticultural industries'*) and a grass sample to one of the dairy feed companies who will analyse it.

In order to grow a good quality crop of veg on this land I would approach it by first trying to create some good quality soil. This takes time as it takes the soil time to assimilate anything put into it. The factors that govern this process are quality of compost, quantity, temperature, moisture, air and method of cultivation and finally time! For these reasons I think that all the land that you wish to grow on should be prepared now! If you end up with too much land prepared you have the option of growing some fodder beet for the animals to supplement their diet as the grass is of very poor quality and seems to have some form of disease – probably 'Rust'.

Although it is in a very poor state at present, the grass that is currently growing will thrive if fed, therefore it needs to be killed off in the growing area as it is very hard to weed amongst veg.

The Timetable

Rotavate grass first @ 1" then @ 2" (spray 500)

Muck spread @ 20–30 tons per acre

Plough to about 6–7" (any deeper and you will ensile the grass waste)

If cloddy, roll when moisture permits, work soil with spring tines (light tractor to avoid start @ 2" and work down to 6" compaction)

Spring tines will work to pull the soil apart and mix

rotavated sod. If you use the rotovator you will damage the soil structure, but a power harrow may work (I've never used one)

Or you can apply 500 + birch pit prep each time you work the soil. <u>All this needs to be done by 3rd week of October!</u>

The land then will need dividing into the two plots:
1. To be planted with over wintering crops and take early spring planting
2. Late spring and summer planting

Plot 1 – Should have autumn beds made up and early spring beds ridged on tractor wheeling like so:– ridge, ridge, bed. Tractor wheel width should be 52″ (*these beds were temporary raised beds formed by ridging soil up to a few inches high*).

This will ensure higher soil temp, better drainage, and incorporation of FYM (*Farmyard Manure*) and better weathering of the soil and ridges.

Plot 2 – After working down put field beans in and leave.

Plot 1 – Bed planted with broad beans, peas, garlic. All this should be done by the 1st week in November. It would also be wise to prepare the polytunnel area so that when it is up the land will be ready.

It would also be good to get the propagation poly up ASAP and get started raising spring cabbage, winter salad and spinach etc.

Re: Propagation of crops and planting
We need to know the proposed end for the veg as this will determine the order of planting etc. Do you wish to

extend the season? How regular will the harvest be and for what purpose?

I.e., number of persons for veg boxes or a market stall, what propagation of the crops will be the low input – i.e. carrots and spuds, and what high input soft fruits, salad leaves, baby veg etc.

Each decision that is made now influences the result. As the veg is probably the area where the project will interface with the community it should be carefully thought about.

If you sit behind a stall with good spuds, carrots, onions and cabbage they will sell. If you do the same with soft fruits, spinach, salad bags, herbs, baby veg etc. then it will buzz!

If we are going for the second option then we need to think now about seed, propagation, potting and compost, the nursery beds, irrigation, cloches, cropping plans etc.

Andy Trim

I loved the confident expertise of this. It was exactly the degree of detail and commitment I had hoped for, in, on the whole, language I understood and felt at ease with. Yet it made my head spin. So much to do! Such absolute deadlines, depths of soil and formations! And although I guessed that '500' or 'birch pit prep' were something to do with biodynamics, I had no idea what. The realities of a commercial operation seemed wholly at odds with nurturing the two or three twenty-minute bursts of rather chaotic activity which was all we had managed to draw from the group in any one day. I knew that Andy eschewed all subsidies. He lived off what he earned and that was entirely dependent on a degree of success in the market. But was that attitude compatible with what we were doing in our stumbling, clumsy way? I was growing to accept the sensation of being constantly out of my depth but the waters ahead seemed endless.

29/9/05

Apparently blood has been found on the floor of the portaloo. Razor's dog was seen waiting outside for ages whilst he was inside at lunchtime on Tuesday. The blood was found immediately after that. It almost certainly means that he used – which would account for the difference in his behaviour – but not perhaps for the sanctimonious little speech about not wanting to upset his mother.

I talk to Rocky about this. Razor cannot come back. If we condone anything of this sort and the others – or the public – find out then we have had it. Rocky agreed to tell him that he is out.

One down. First failure.

30/9/05

Things go from bad to worse.

Whilst filming GW I get a phone call from the production team to say that Martin Bateman had been found dead in his parents' bathroom with a syringe still in his leg. It is thought that it was a drug overdose but this cannot be confirmed until the coroner's report.

He was twenty-three.

October 2005

Martin had just come out of prison on remand and was was due to go to court in October over an assault case. He knew that if found guilty – and the only doubt was not whether he had done it or not but whether the victim would turn up in court – he faced 5–7 years in prison. He was apparently deeply remorseful and depressed about this. The case had dragged on for a long time but it was not the first time that he had been involved in this kind of violent crime. He had form.

I read that in 2001 Martin and a friend, Daniel Byrne, both aged nineteen, had invited another man, Stephen Edwards, to join them for a drink. Later that night they took him to an area of Worcester City centre known as The Arches where they attacked him, kicking him and hitting him on the head with a bottle. Battered and bleeding they then marched him to a cashpoint, but his account was overdrawn and the machine did not release any money. They scene at the bank was filmed on a CCTV camera. Both men admitted robbery and were sent to detention for three years. Martin, apparently the father of a three-year-old daughter, was also ordered to complete 92 days of a previous sentence imposed for wounding.

I then discovered there were other, more recent offences.

In January 2004, Martin was charged with driving while under the influence of both cocaine and methadone. Two months later he was picked up by police, driving the day after he had been banned in court for 18 months. As a result he was charged with eight motoring offences, which included driving without insurance or a MoT certificate. The defending solicitor in this case urged the court to give Martin a drug treatment order rather than a custodial sentence. It was encouraging to read that he recognised Martin's problems as stemming from drug use, and hoped that there might be 'some light at the end of the tunnel' if he could be helped to come off them.

Martin's behaviour over the previous few months had been tricky and I remembered him at the farm we visited when he was catatonic. He was certainly no angel and a handful at the best of times. But it was hard to think ill or even judgementally about the dead. He had charm and I remember on the first visit to Monkland he was the one who showed most enthusiasm and asked most questions. He was a big, lumbering lad but Rocky told me that he was a really good footballer. The film crew that spent time with him at home and in Worcester said that it was impossible for him to walk down the street without recognising and greeting or being greeted by someone every few yards. He had presence.

I had no idea that he was a father of what would now be a seven-year-old daughter.

We talked about his death when we met up on the Tuesday. They were surprisingly dismissive and apparently unaffected by it. They had seen it all before. People use gear, people die. I asked them if it would put them off at all.

Not really Kate said. She was clearly very upset but this seemed to harden her, put up her defences even higher than normal.

We all know people that have died through using she said. I've got a friend with one leg cos she had gangrene from using and she's still shooting into the groin of the other one. Probably have that cut off too. Nothing stops you.

We agreed to plant a tree for him and I suggested an apple because it would bear fruit and a Worcester Pearmain because Martin came from Worcester.

Martin'd be glad it was food Kate said, cos he was always a greedy bugger.

03.10.05

Martin!
I know your not here but you'll never be far away in my thoughts and in my heart. You were/are a top mate yeah. I'm going to miss you so much. WHY?? Thats what I keep saying to myself. WHAT IF? But at the end of the day you're never coming back. I will never forget you, always in my thoughts. Love you and miss you forever. Your mate Katie.
Love you mate xx Katie xxxxx

I had ordered twelve pallets so that we could make compost bins but they arrived as we were leaving so the group made them up the next day whilst I was in London doing radio interviews for a book that was just being published and taking part in BBC 1's 'Celebrity Mastermind'. I have always had a general policy to avoid any kind of event or broadcast with 'celebrity' in its title but did this because it was an opportunity to promote the project and John Humphrys duly asked me about it when my turn came. Spoke about Martin's death and instantly regretted it as it felt as though I was parading it for shock value. Which I was.

While I was in London there was apparently another big bust-up centred around Tom and food. He seems to see a meal that is put before him as a challenge to his independence. Why are you making me eat this? Why should I? I can eat what I like thank you etc., etc. Apparently it got very heavy and unpleasant for everyone – not least for Tom.

05.10.05

Today I have reached the end of my tether and feel like I don't want to come back here again. I seriously don't want any more hassle so the best way to stop it is not come back. I have enjoyed myself up until now but I will not be treated like a CUNT because it is not on.

Tom

I would like jacket potatoes, fish fingers (beans baked), chips, mash potatoes, tuna pasta, sweetcorn, mayonnaise.

Katie

A brilliant morning's work making the compost bins. I felt proud to be part of the project and everyone enjoyed themselves. Worked hard and we laughed together until lunch then sadly the food issue kicked off once again – we have to think more about what we are doing here and trying to achieve. Keep up the good work.

Rocky

10/10/05

I went to a steering group meeting composed of locals split between those most vehemently for the project and those most strongly against it. The main concern, as I am now getting used to, was protecting themselves against the possible ravages of the group's drug-crazed rampages. So most of the time is spent stressing how unwell and unfocused they are and the last people that you would choose to go on a good rampage. As with all meetings it is tedious and lasts at least three times too long.

Ironic that this message is appended to the daybook for last week:

Message for Monty from Katie and Andrés. 'We both feel safe on the farm'.

Rocky

11/10/05

Spent all day with the group on the land. It is a lovely autumn so far, softly sunny and warm. A pleasure to be outside all day. But there is so much infrastructure stuff to be done. We don't have water, cover, machinery, place for animals, fences – nothing really other than a bare field.

We have had 30 tons cow manure delivered and Philip spread a lot of it onto the grass ready for cultivating into the ground. However, the machine threw it indiscriminately and most of it was deposited as a thick layer over the area that is marked out for a path. So we all shovelled, raked and scraped it up and threw it over the right piece of ground.

But the tractor – a loan from Kubota organised by Marsha – arrived to great excitement along with rotavator attachment, front loader and trailer. Kubota, of course, know that as we are being filmed for a year the chances of it appearing in the programme – repeatedly – are almost certain. No such thing as a free lunch. But I don't care at all. I am happy to be used and to use in this way if it enables us to operate. Tom and Chris immediately took ownership. Andrés showed no interest at all and Kate resented the boys' blokishness about it. Andy B, as ever, stands to one side, semi-detached. But despite being bright orange in a landscape of tawny grass and foliage, it is a good thing both for getting them all engaged and for practical use. Given the response in the daybook I am sure that they would rather have had it at the beginning instead of the team of shire horses.

11.10.05

Having a good time so far. Learning about how to work the
tractor and I apologized for my behaviour to everyone speak to
you soon before we go home.

Tom

All round a good day. It was a SHIT start in all sense of the
word cos we were shoveling it for an hour but driving the
tractor was all good.

Chris

Today is different and better than staying at home. Time has
passed quick. I find it hard to work with others.

Andrew B

12/10/05

Today would have been Martin's twenty-fourth birthday.

I picked up the Worcester Pearmain (which Marsha had huge
problems in getting hold of) from Paul Jasper in Leominster and
took it over for the tree planting. Martin's family came – grandmother, brothers, parents and Martin's girlfriend and his two
children. One brother couldn't come because he was in prison. All
were friendly and unsolemn but serious and slightly awkward.
They were all dressed like Martin and all looked a little like him.
This was, in a curious way, disturbing. It began to rain.

Kate, normally slouched and huddled against cold, work and
world, had dressed up and acted as the hostess showing great
dignity and grace. Tom energetically helped me dig the hole for
the little tree and I said a few words about Martin living on
through the project and the tree which would, in its time, bear

fruit and hopefully go on doing so for all our lifetimes and beyond. This is how a village priest must feel. Part deadly serious, part hopeless fraud.

We all ate sandwiches and talked about Martin and looked at pictures of him. Then they went off to visit the son inside. Martin's funeral is on Friday but I cannot go as I shall be filming 'Gardeners' World'. At least that was what I said to his parents, Rocky and myself. The truth was that I knew that if I went I would be accompanied by a film crew and I dreaded the way that might draw attention away from Martin and his family. Perhaps they would have liked it. I don't know.

But I do know that I've got to carry on now. It's life and death.

12.10.05

I am so thankful for the owners of the land who have let all the youngsters come to work and learn about the countryside. I wish there were so many more who could help in this way. And a very big thank you for giving my son the chance. He did enjoy it. Also thank you for the lovely service on his birthday and the planting of his apple tree,

E Bateman

PS thanks to all the friends.

It has been a very nice day today. I met Martin's family and they all seemed in good spirits considering. We planted a tree for Martin and Trish made a lovely lunch. Cheers all.

Chris.

Today was really special! Went really well and Martin's family were holding out. Planted the tree. Everyone scoffed loads so Martin would have liked it.

Katie

On this day of the plantation of Martin's tree I feel
overwhelmed and cheerful as I know that his life will continue
on as will his tree. The countryside is a place you feel free so I
know that Martin is free to all this. From your brother R
Bateman. PS with all my love and respect.

October continued. The weather changed and my own tendency
to gloom kicked in. I can remember no sunshine for the re-
mainder of the year. But we had to keep plugging on. We were
busy on the farm and behind the scenes, trying to organise
equipment, visits to local woods, buy some cattle (which is still
yet to happen) and to make some sense out of the anarchy of
actually managing the project. There were weekly requests from
journalists to visit us, write about the story with the shadow of
Monkland still on us. How were we doing? Had we alienated the
locals? Behind the media fascination was the lure of the freak-
show and the underlying assumption that the group were somehow 'other'. The last thing we needed was any kind of publicity.
So I banned any contact with the media, rang a few journalists to
promise them access in the spring and tried to create a safe, low-
key atmosphere at the Rock. I was determined that time and
energy should be put into this group on a quiet, day-by-day,
basis.

A solar tunnel arrived and we slowly put it up over three days
despite the incomprehensibility of the instructions. The only way
it could happen was to work in a team.

Philip brought in one of his huge contractor's bits of kit to
power-rotavate the ground and I ordered beans and garlic ready to
be planted in November. The power-rotavating turned out to be a
mistake. I should have taken more note of Andy Trim's advice. As
soon as it was done the weather turned and it rained every day,
turning the soil to a bog floating above a pan of hard clay.

As the weather limited the work that we could do outside the
mess hut became increasingly important and I bought a camping

stove, cups, cutlery etc., to try and make it feel as domestic as possible. Food continued to be a problem for everyone.

Tom got worse and continued to find conflict at every turn. One or two of the others say that he is smoking a lot of crack, which doesn't help. He also has medication for his anxiety which he says he forgets or omits to take. Whatever the reason it is as though he becomes possessed with paranoia and anxiety. Any criticism or comment about the group was taken as a personal attack thinly disguised by being addressed at the group. Why wasn't I man enough to come out and say it directly to him? He knew what I was fucking thinking. What did I take him for? A cunt?

Although he raves and strides about in his anger (it is actually more distress than anger) I don't feel any physical fear of him but on the other hand don't really trust what he might do. I suppose I feel up to dealing with him physically should the need arise. But psychologically and emotionally I feel hopelessly inadequate and unable to help him. In between the outbursts he is still the Tom who is vulnerable and open and eminently likeable.

As ever, the daybook holds its own tantalisingly incomplete but telling story.

19.10.05

Yes, yes OK. It was me who graffitied the bog. Really sorry wont happen again and I'll clean it off. Sorry again.

Chris xx

Really good day. No crack since Saturday 15.10.05 doing well really finding it hard. Today we put the poly tunnel up with a lot of teamwork. Phillip, Rocky, David and PC Mudaway done really well. PC Mudaway was a visitor from Staffordshire Police and came to see how we run our project

Katie xx

Our four Tamworth pigs arrived and we made them an enclosure. Katie took one look at them and said 'Oh they're too big!' and walked away. She had not catered for the fact that piglets grow. But they seemed sweet enough to me. But then I love pigs. Thirty years ago I worked on a factory pig farm in Hampshire. It was horrific and deeply demeaning. I desperately needed the job so stuck it out for three miserable months before finally summoning the moral fibre to walk out. Despite what amounted to systematic, cynical torture, it engendered a love for pigs – although I did not eat bacon for a few years after that and I have never knowingly eaten mass-produced bacon since. They are highly intelligent, social animals that add warmth to any farm. I also love ham, pork and bacon and hoped that rearing the piglets to the stage of going to the butcher and then eating meat that we had lovingly reared would be the first connection to the true rhythms and cycles of the food they eat.

25.10.05

Came today to finish the poly-tunnel but apart from that it is not too interesting. Feeling really down today.

Bye for nye. Tom Allen

A miserable day weather wise. Our pigs arrived and we made the pen to house them. We sorted out the sliding doors on the polydome. Monty and Tom are rowing yet again over food yet again and I don't think it will get resolved. But I'm fine and all is well. Only if it stopped bloody raining

Chris

Today has made me realise that you have to take the rough with the smooth but people have to realise that some of us have grown up around arguments and violence and do not appreciate any confrontations that go on. So please for the sake of those people, do not have confrontations!

Thanx, all the best.

Katiexxxxxx

Our pigs arrived so yet another move forward. The doors are on the polytunnel so all round a good working day – food issues raised their head yet again but hopefully it is all part of the process of change. (We just have to judge the speed of change) but we are all still together, still motivated and still fired up to come back again next week. We are all going to be THE LAST MAN STANDING !!!!!!

Rocky

November 2005

This is where we came in.

1/11/05

I went to Ludlow first thing and bought bread, drinks, bacon, lots of buns and cakes, salad, fruit etc. All organic, local and satisfying my foodie sensibilities. Cost about fifty quid. Ludlow is, of course, the foodie capital of England. It has three Michelin starred restaurants (two now since Sean Hill has shut up shop) and fulfils exactly the mixture of sophisticated expertise and detail about food that comes from quarter of a century of modern travel and increasing wealth, together with a Georgian and medieval rural charm that is only found in central and southern English small rural towns and villages. A marriage of John Betjeman and Elizabeth David. Ten miles down the road Leominster has two Indian restaurants, one of which is not bad at all. I am sure that I could have bought the same volume and probably calories for a third as much at some cut-price supermarket. I am certain that the group would have been just as happy.

Then on to the Rock.

Kate was rattling. Sick. Shaking. Her misery infects everything. The others solicitous but they have seen – and been – it all before.

So in the last month:

Martin dead.

Lee and Wayne in prison (Wayne sentenced just four days before finishing his order. Although it is entirely in keeping with a well trod path there is something hopelessly depressing about it). Wayne also has an embolism from injecting heroin.

Kate hopelessly unable to control her addiction and desperately ill.

Rocky wrote in the daybook:

Yesterday 31 October 2005 we lost Wayne to a 4 month custodial sentence (96 hours before he finished his order). I do hope Wayne will get himself sorted in prison, come out clean and with some positive thoughts over what to do with his life. He got good support at the court from Katie, Tom & Chris.

Today on the farm we have Andy P, Andy B and Katie. Moved the pigs and all had a good chat and worked on the compost bins. This afternoon it's the polytunnel I believe. Andy P is becoming the comedian and stealing my jokes. He will have to spend more time locked in the car!

Rocky

I'm enjoying today. I feel sorry for Katie. Have got to help her out and all stick together as a team.

Andy P

Not very positive today. Hope better next week. I feel weak, very weak. I got work when I finish here. Painting a kitchen 3–4 hours work.

Andy B

2/11/05

I write all morning but go over after lunch. They are leaving almost as I arrive but I stay long enough for a cup of tea and chat.

Kate bright and happy. It turned out that Andrés went and got her a bag of heroin and she used last night. It is extraordinary how well it makes her seem.

Tom announces that all he wants is death and oblivion.

They have made four raised beds for the tunnel and dug and manured two of them. This amounts to real achievement and they show me their work with real pride.

4/11/05

Kate rings me at Berryfields whilst I am filming 'Gardeners' World' to tell me that she has a clean crack sample. The knock-on effects of this are momentous. Her script had been reduced following the government's policy – which I find inexplicable – of reducing methadone if the user fails three consecutive drug tests (the tests are done every Monday and Friday). As a result the user has greater incentive to replace the opiate that came from methadone with street heroin. So the situation inevitably spirals from bad to worse. The reduction of the script is supposed to act as an incentive to put in clean samples so that it can be taken back up again but this is completely counter-intuitive. Addicts don't think or act in that rational, structured way. They want gear and they want it now. Addicts like Kate use crack and heroin in combination – one to take you up and one to bring you back down. It is usually much easier to avoid one if you stay away from the other. By giving a clean sample it means that her script is increased to 40 ml. That in turn means that she will not need – or hopefully desire – heroin. She is jubilant.

8/11/05

Kate, Andrés, Deaf Andy and Tom. It is a lovely morning – clear blue sunshine after rain, but unbelievably muddy – rain almost constantly over the past week and the place slipping and sliding under our feet. When we arrive David and Philip are busy fixing insulation in the mess room. The result is a messy mess room so hard to make breakfast for everyone.

The pigs have turned their lovely grassy paddock into a quagmire. They run squealing when Andrés approaches with food and sit like happy hounds when you scratch them. The two boars are appreciably bigger than the sows and more docile.

David has typed up a list of rules to control mud. I read these out and happen to look at Tom when talking about clearing up the mess from cleaning the tractor. He explodes into a fit of paranoiac outrage. It is a bad start. His face is covered in sores and scratches. Rocky asks me to 'be gentle with him. He is not in a good way.' I'll say.

We double dig the remaining two raised beds which is hot hard work. I do one with Tony – a new driver, retired but fit and pleasantly unfazed although clearly bemused by every aspect of what he finds himself in the middle of – fetching the muck and Philip and Andrés do the other one with me getting the muck. I take in the rotavator and Deaf Andy rotavates the beds dug last week. This makes a mess but keeps him happy. While we work outside, Kate refuses to come out into the cold but tidies the mess room – which she does very well.

Lunch is taken with great decorum. It is chicken pie – which Kate has specially requested. Tricia – who is really not at all well with an attack of Lupus – makes a delicious one. Kate won't touch it and says that it ain't chicken pie. This is because she has found some bacon in it.

That's not right is it? It's not proper chicken pie with bacon. I can't eat that!

Andrés – ordinarily the best eater – hardly touches his food. He says he does not feel great. Deaf Andy says he wants pork pie. It happens I have bought some on my way in. I am angry with him and, unusually, push him for politeness. He genuinely does not know what I am talking about.

In the afternoon Marsha arrives with mipex (a woven plastic layer used to lay under gravel or wood chip paths to stop weeds pushing through) to lay around the tunnel. But the heavens open and water pours off the roof down and *inside* the tunnel. More quagmire. Andrés and I make a raised bed in the rain outside but get truly soaked. We pack it all in. They leave happily enough except for Tom.

The raised beds are an important part of the layout on this very heavy clay soil. The ones in the polytunnel and immediately outside are essentially wood-edged frames with extra soil added. In the tunnel this soil is barrowed in but outside it comes from the topsoil of the paths between each raised bed. The idea is that once dug and manured you never need dig them again as long as you do not stand on them or compact them in any way. It also means that all cultivation and weeding is focused on the specific growing area and that the soil drains better and heats up quicker. They are hard work to make – ideally they should all be double dug – but save a huge amount of time and energy even over a period as short as our lease.

08.11.05

I woke up at 6.45am this morning because I had to walk $3\frac{1}{2}$ miles from Great Comberton to Pershore. It took me 25 minutes to walk because I was stopping at my mother's house. I got up early to get this Project. I did this by myself with no help whatsoever. That's my first time without asking others to get me up or getting someone to take me to Pershore. I was very positive today and I did it. I can prove I can do things without involving other people. I'm very glad.

Monty is very good to work with. Very easy and understandable person and Rocky is brilliant because he's not a cop no more. I bet before he was not as good as now because he was only doing his job but I know he's sound. A way to go Rocky, keep it up!

Andy Breakwell

Thank you Andy, this job is hard and comments like above make it much easier and worthwhile.

Rocky

Have been working hard today. I feel really good in myself. Hope Kate is OK.

Andy P

It is only since transcribing the daybook that I understand what Andy B was saying when he commented that I was '*good to work with. Very easy and understandable person*'. Andy is very deaf. I have a loud voice and tend to look straight at people when I talk to them. That means he can hear/lip read me better than most.

9/11/05

Gloriously sunny day. Floods all over Herefordshire. Up all night. My stomach is in revolt. Feel a wreck.

I get fish and chips on my way over at lunchtime. Tom, Chris, Kate, Andrés and new person, Barrie, are there. I shake Barrie's hand and he half offers a limp token, looking bemused, as though he has never done it before. He is Lee's best friend. Twenty-five but looks sixteen. His left hand is heavily bandaged. This means he does no work at all whilst I am there but sits on a pallet and watches us. Says he has cracked addiction but is on 70 ml of methadone a day which also means he has a substantial heroin habit too (the greater the methadone dosage the greater the previous heroin consumption. Anything over 50 ml implies a hefty habit).

Tom has been moaning about lack of lunch (the table groans with pies, cheese, biscuits, rolls) and greets me, bearing fish and chips, like a saviour. But then he eats nothing. Chris will not speak and eats nothing. Kate nibbles. But the others eat and the pigs love the ensuing leftovers.

They have laid a land drain along the edge of the tunnel and started to dig out a hole to join the big drain running down the field. I take over this and dig down for an hour or so. I get down so the hole is almost over my head but still no sign of a drain. In the end, about 6ft down in pure clay, we decide to put the pipe in and refill with stone, which we do. Only Andrés helps with this. Tom and Chris put up the punch bag that I have brought in specifically to use up some of their aggression and play no part in the work.

Barry sits and watches. Kate chats. Then just before we refill she produces a crack pipe in a bag and asks me to bury it in the hole. The pipe is metal and rather beautiful.

Are you sure? I ask with inappropriate politeness, as though she were offering me a cutting from the garden or a home-made cake.

Go on, just bury the fucker she says. Stick it in the ground.

She can always dig a six-foot hole in the mud and rain if she wants it back Rocky says.

I stick it down at my feet and start back-filling with gravel before she can change her mind. It feels a very significant moment.

Tom tells me that the marks all over his face are from violent scratching when taking crack. He says he needs to talk to someone but there is no one. What about his girl? I say.

I can't talk to her about feelings. It's not fair.

They have been together for thirteen years. Childhood sweethearts. He is twenty-one and she twenty.

They leave at 3.45 with Chris complaining about being kept

waiting. He gives nothing – hardly seems an addict and has none of the apparent vulnerability of the others although apparently has been a heavy user of heroin and crack. A tough cookie.

After they go the BBC crew and I are shellshocked and agree that Tom is a walking disaster about to happen and that we can hardly continue with him. I have an absolute sensation that something very bad is waiting to happen. I need to speak to Rocky/probation about him.

Drive home into the setting sun on the flooded fields with six dirty eggs rolling on the seat next to me.

When I next saw the daybook I realised that my reading of Chris was, not for the first time, inaccurate and incomplete.

09.11.05

I'm having a very bad day. I've been rowing with Katie and I wish people could just leave me alone. I don't think I can keep coming here any more. I don't think this is what I need at this time in my life. It's all a bit too much. Sorry everyone!!!

Chris

Rocky, as ever, not only understood exactly what was going on but managed to write it where it mattered, as a message to them in the daybook:

I do not pretend to know how you all feel but I do understand that each of you has a mixed bag of emotions and when there are 5 of you on the farm that just creates an atmosphere of chaos especially when my emotions are added as well!

When you get down please think of the bare field and the scruffy untidy open fronted shed that greeted us when we first arrived and look at it now! The alterations are your achievements – go back 12 months – did any of you think you would be doing anything like this?

Life is full of ups and downs. It was difficult today when we all seemed down. Do not forget as Monty tells us, this is a bad time of the year on the farm because nothing can be planted so we may wonder sometimes what we are doing out there but little things are being built all the time. Goodnight diary, sleep well.

Rocky

10/11/05

Lie awake half the night thinking about Tom. I feel totally out of my depth and ill-equipped to help him. Realise that I don't *have* to. I have a constant fear that I will get a phone call saying something drastic has happened. This is probably absurdly melodramatic and influenced by the finality and shock of Martin's death, but the thought is there. He is not a violent person and is apparently a good father and kind to his girlfriend. But he exudes unpredictability and chaos. But maybe he is using the safety of myself and David to rail against us – knowing that no real harm can be done. Maybe we are the safety valve that enables him to be the loving and kind partner and father that he undoubtedly can be and wants to be.

I dunno. I really do not know.

Decide that I can admit defeat. That it is too much for us. That I am untrained without much clue as to what he is doing and that some things – most things – are beyond me. That the things that I *can* do are being severely compromised by him and that the whole group feels charged with his distress. That he is a bad influence on Chris and makes Andrés silent and withdrawn. That I always keep an eye on the kitchen knife when he is about and prepare myself to disarm or overpower him. That this is completely beyond me.

One of the problems with Tom is that he apparently doesn't take the medication offered him nor attend psychiatric sessions organised for him. I decide – with the clock satisfyingly reading a red digital 3.33 on the ceiling in the dark – that I will not have him there until he has had regular psychiatric help – maybe only if he has attended one that week and only after a break – say till Christmas.

I know that it will confirm Tom's paranoia and make him feel angry and bitter at the rejection. No one comes out very well.

Huge sense of failure accompanied by relief.

Having made the decision I sent the following email to the chief probation officer, David Chantler.

Subject: Tom

I am very concerned about the mental state of Tom (I am ashamed to say that I do not know his surname) from the project.

He has always been the most disturbed and troubled of the group and that condition seems to have become much worse over the past month or so. It seems to me that he is on the point of some damaging actions to himself or others. It is clear that he needs urgent and frequent psychiatric help. He has reacted with violent anger to myself and David on a number of occasions and his paranoia makes any reasonable debate impossible. The result is that his presence is threatening and disturbing without any sense of progression or that we are providing him with any comfort or hope.

His participation is definitely damaging to the group and I do not believe that it is helping him in any meaningful way – other than perhaps taking him out of an environment for a few hours once or twice a week where he would be using drugs – and on that score he admits to bingeing on crack and heroin over the past few weeks.

In short I feel that the project does not offer him what he needs and we are all inadequately equipped to deal with his specific demands. He is taking up a place that might be much better suited to someone who actively wants to be there and benefit from it.

I would suggest removing him immediately for a period of a month or two to see if a) he improves and b) the group dynamism benefits. I would welcome him back when a psychiatric report suggested that he was ready for it and when he himself felt willing and ready to re-enter on our terms.

I have talked around this with Rocky but not directly in these terms. I will ring him over the next 24 hours to discuss it.

Other than this real progress is being made – albeit of a minute, painful, disturbing, exhausting, depressing and utterly demanding nature.

best wishes
Monty

Having sent the email I make myself a cup of tea and look at some pictures of the group taken when the shire horses came to plough. The sky is blue. They are all a bit cowed, a bit sullen and corralled but one of the group stands out as being particularly photogenic and handsome.

It is Tom.

Tom has not been to the Rock since that day although as I write this he is due to join us for a barbecue to celebrate our first year of the project. Rocky has kept in touch with him and he is apparently doing well. I remember that he once said to me that what he really wanted was a job in which he could drive a tractor all day in a big field and just be left to get on with it on his own. The opposite of what we were trying to do but it perfectly fits the modern farming contractor.

I have always felt bad about him. We failed. There is no other gloss to be put on it. But when I said this to Rocky he pointed out that maybe Tom needed the crisis and failure of his time on the project to get to the point where he could change. Maybe we could not do it for him but we could act as the catalyst for him to do it himself. By all accounts things have – are – changing for the better for him. I wish him nothing but happiness and success and that the trouble in his mind might be eased.

I would try and spend one whole day and part of another with them at the Rock, fitting it in around filming and writing commitments. When I was not there the daybook would tell me not so much what had happened but how their individual worlds were faring.

15.11.05

Well, today has got to have been one of the best days so far. I feel we've all worked hard together and I even got to have a long go on the tractor. Only downfall is I got to clean the bastard! Rocky has been a real mate today and I don't know what we would all do without him. Cheers Rock.

Chris

Well I feel a bit lost today. Trying to keep myself occupied. Hope Kate is OK. Hope things go OK for her. Looking forward to tomorrow.

Andrés Pope

I'm still trying but I don't like it. There's no Monty, it's just Rocky, Phil, Chris, Andy P and me. We did drain the polytunnel so I'm trying, I am really trying. I'm not good in a group. I've never had it just something I was brought up with. Since the

past I don't want a friend because what happened for the last
12–13 years ago. I've been ripped off, bullied, mugged, abused.
It's hard to trust anyone yet I find it hard to open up

   PS Give us a bit of time, I will get there I promise because
trusting people is hard because when you've been let down so
many times I was going to give up but I don't want to give up,
it's not me.

Andy Breakwell

16/11/05

Andy B comes in huddled and shivering. He says that he is cold
because he spent last night at his grandmother's house rather
than the car. I must look blank. He explains that the cold is all
right till you get warm. That spoils you.

> SHIT (sorry for language). Started to feel so cold because been
> in a very warm house last night because I stayed at my Nan's.
> Something inside me says I shouldn't come today but I'm sure
> that wont last as soon as I work. I all the way feel like it when I
> arrive somewhere. I did not have no gear last night that's why I
> feel like this now. I see how I feel dinner time.

Andy Breakwell

We sow our first garlic and broad beans in pots because the
ground is so wet. I try and make this into an event – tara! seeds in
the ground! This is what it is all about! Seeds of hope! They eye
me with a mixture of suspicion and sorrow, exactly as my
children do. But, unlike my children, they patiently and faithfully
do as I do and many hands makes remarkably light work of it.
Too light in fact. There is not much else that we can do.

Today we have planted our first seeds – beans and garlic. I feel OK today, a little bit down when I start to think of things but working helps clear the mind.

Andy Pope

22/11/05

Freezing fog. Thermometer says minus four. Most of the day is a huddle against the cold. I took along the four blackcurrant bushes that I potted up last January in readiness for the project and which have sat outside the greenhouse at home for nearly a year. We plant them up at the top. Feels ceremonial.

Andy B, who spends half his time in his own silent world, can be very talkative although conversations with him are difficult. In a group he will come out with *non sequiturs* that are so exquisitely timed it is hard not to believe that he has waited and inserted them for maximum effect. But he swears that this is not the case. He just cannot hear a babble of voices. His daybook entries are often longer and more confessional than the others and take him a long time to write, crouched intensely over the page.

22.11.05

First day of the week, it's very cold, fog coming down slowly. I wish I stayed at home in a way cos it's cold but I came. We'll just see what happens. Even I look better. I don't feel it. I hope I feel better as the day goes by by looking at everyone. They look very positive today. I feel that's why I hate winter because my hearing is terrible this time of year. I will sort it out by getting a hearing aid. I'll make an appointment this week. Without them I miss out a lot that's why I feel left out but it's my fault. If I wasn't bullied for it, I wouldn't have a problem. I probably be wearing them now? But somehow I shouldn't give a shit what people think but it's the camera what bothers me but without my hearing aid I don't half miss out a lot.

Andy B

Later

I feel better today because I'm better when one to one. It's more easy to understand and you don't have to worry if no-one takes the piss of ya because it makes me feel better because of the past. I am trying to forget the past and look forward but when we had rough times you avoid it so that's why I avoid groups. That's what happened in the past because whether I wrong people starts or I'm right they started that's why I lean my back against the wall.

Andy

29/11/05

We went to the Mistletoe sale at Tenbury which is just a couple of miles down the road from the Rock. This part of North Herefordshire, on the border with Shropshire and Wales, is the heart of mistletoe country. It grows in great cloudy balls in every orchard and hedgerow. But this is potentially its last year as the auction site, right in the middle of the little town, has been bought and is to be developed. Buyers come from all over the country to buy bundles of holly and mistletoe to sell anywhere from street corners to department stores. Most of it is gathered by local gypsy families – and has been done so for a very long time – but it is also an important piece of Christmas revenue for local farmers and their wives who make wreaths for the sale. It is held on three consecutive weeks starting with the last Tuesday in November.

Until relatively recently each village round here performed fertility rites in the new year that seemed to involve burning balls of hawthorn and mistletoe that had been picked the previous year and drinking cider until you fell over. A new sprig of mistletoe was placed over the door where it remained for the rest of the year.

It was the first time that I had seen this lot off the farm, out in the world as the original group – Martin, Lee, Razor, Wayne, Adam and Tom had died, gone to prison, got a job or proved beyond us. The single most obvious thing is how they stand out. They are the norm on the farm but out in the world they are paler, iller, shiftier than everyone else. Their clothes – baseball caps, white trainers, tracksuit bottoms – instantly set them apart from the ruddy-faced, jerseyed, wellied, becoated crowd. Andrés, who I think of as slowish, pensive and deliberate was instantly street smart, moving fast, feral, working the place expertly – finding out what went on, who was in charge and generally sussing the system. Kate, on the other hand, so bossy and assured in her own territory, huddled into herself and looked out of her depth.

The mistletoe prices were high – up to £70 a bundle. (There is no objective measurement for this. The bundles are of no set size. Prospective buyers lift them, feel the weight and sometimes measure it with spring scales, and compare them all for quality before deciding how much they are prepared to pay.)

We go back to the farm for lunch full of grand money-making schemes. They plan to collect mistletoe on the way home.

We could get a fair few bundles in your car Rocky, specially if we squeezed up a bit.

Kate, at least, has not quite grasped the concept of ownership of growing things.

How can it belong to a farmer if it's growing on a fucking tree? For fuck's sake! It's only branches!

They also see the proceeds of any resulting sale as cash that will go into their pockets. I point out that it will be a harvest and go into the communal pot.

Fuck that! That's my Christmas presents money.

Oh yeah. I am learning to be cynical. The best laid plans of an addict *always* gan astray. It would be a present to self. X bags of gear. Happy Christmas.

December 2005

Beginning of December. It is a cold, crisp morning. Blue sky. A surprising amount of leaves remain on the trees but the landscape has been filleted, ransacked.

Andrés and I are turning the compost heap. I chide him for being a bit slow and dreamy. He says that he had a bad night. I tell him that working up a sweat will do him more good than anything else. He smiles ruefully.

Tony urges him to tell me what happened last night. Go on I say. What happened? Andrés reluctantly tells me that as he was going back into his hostel with a friend who lives on the streets (why? He's an alcoholic. No one can help him) another street-living drunk, much older, sidles up and says to his friend that 'all your friends are leaving you now. I'll come back and get you later on.' Andrés said 'I couldn't be having that.' So he spent the night on the street with his friend to protect him. No sleeping bag, no coat, minus 3 and dossing on a concrete bench. Then he walked to the pick-up point for Rocky – no breakfast – and came here. As he tells me this he does not stop turning the compost heap.

Another day he is walking to meet Rocky, eight in the morning and he bumps into a friend who owes him £10. This friend suggests that instead of the cash he could be repaid with a bag of gear. Imagine the temptation for a junkie. Andrés said that he literally ran away down the street.

We spend a morning driving around the countryside looking for good mistletoe and then knocking on the owners' door asking if we can cut some. This involves a school for foreign students –

101

which is a surreal thing to find in the Herefordshire winter countryside – and an extremely friendly old farmer. We don't get much but enough in all four rather thin bundles.

Collecting mistletoe sparks off dreams of money for Chris, Kate and Andrés. I point out that any sales will go back into the project. They regard this as a form of theft. Nevertheless we gather four bundles (a lot) of mistletoe and prepare it for sale the next week. Andrés is excited by it as a first harvest. Chris coolly competent and as ever, slightly superior in a Jack-the-lad way. Kate bitter, funny, confused.

She says that she used to use to the extent of £300 per week. She had to shoplift between £600 and £1,000 to service that.

She receives £44 per week benefit. She never uses that for buying heroin. She shoplifts for that – and will be triumphant if she has not been lifting the night before because I suppose that means that she hasn't used. She longs for a job but no one will employ her. I wouldn't. But having a criminal record is going to put off all but the most caring employer. At least she is now talking about a job.

But the trouble with a job is that they don't pay you for two weeks so you're more fucking skint than ever. In the past like, when I got a job I had to bloody work to see me through till I got paid.

What do you mean?

I had to lift two weeks worth before I began work to get enough gear to see me through till I got paid. Wasn't worth it. Then I got some skanky sum at the end of it. It's taking the piss.

I discover that the probation service have placed Chris, Andrés and Kate on an OSAP (Office for Substance Abuse Prevention) drug rehabilitation course which takes place on Tuesdays and Thursdays. This means that it clashes with their visits and that they will miss the Mistletoe sale. Rocky says it cannot be altered. The courses run when they run. I try and get the BBC to exert pressure.

Sent: 01 December 2005 12:04
To: Dee Ryding, Series Producer
Subject: Mistletoe and insane planning.

Hi
We had a good couple of days visiting the Holly &
Mistletoe auction in Tenbury where Andrés and Kate
became obsessed with making some money – and Kate
bitterly bemoaning her lack of funds – but thinking of it
in terms of a lack of job rather than the need to do
more shoplifting. On Wednesday we gathered mistletoe
from local farmers who were helpful and encouraging
and the plan is to sell it at the auction next week.

This is exactly the right type of thing for us to be
doing and generating a really positive mood. It is local,
seasonal produce sold at a local market, with the money
going back into the project (we will pay for the
Christmas dinner with it).

But I hear from Rocky today that the drug
programme has been changed to start next Tuesday so
that Chris, Kate & Andrés – the main protagonists –
cannot come to the sale. This seems to me to be a crazy
and destructive piece of unjoined-up thinking. Is there
any way that we can bring pressure to bear to stop this?
Monty

Notice the 'we'. I had long lost track of whose camp I was in. But
it worked. Your licence fee was well spent. A day later I got a
reply from the producer who had organised for Chris, Andrés
and Kate to come to the auction and stay until midday. If Philip
could deliver the mistletoe first thing the auctioneers had agreed
to place our lot early enough to guarantee it appearing by then.
The three would then be driven by the BBC to Worcester for their
course whilst the rest of us would go to back to the Rock.

4/12/05

Talking to an audience at Hay (to promote *My Roots*) there is a huge amount of goodwill for the project. For the first time for ages I think positively about it. I realise that for the past few months it has been like swimming in mud. Necessary, even inevitable, but not much joy.

I listen to Sir Christopher Meyer talk about his book *Washington Confidential* in extreme discomfort. My teeth hurt like hell. This has been a gradually worsening case for the last year or so but is the norm within the group. Their mouths are in constant crisis.

Heroin fucks your teeth up. Research in America has shown that heroin use increases the intensity of craving for sweet foods whilst simultaneously leads to an almost total neglect of dental hygiene. Methadone also dries the mouth up so increases risk of gingivitis and will make a mouth already ravaged by years of heroin a whole lot worse. Most users assuage the thirst of methadone with fizzy drinks and it is also mixed in a sweet syrup that sticks to the rotting teeth. Both make a bad situation worse, leading to what one website calls 'rampant caries' along with a gleeful picture of an explosion of a mouth.

Heroin also masks the pain of toothache in the early stages – so the user will not notice it until the damage is bad. Although I see that a heroin user actually has a lower tolerance to pain and normal analgesics. Only gear works.

Crack is even worse. It causes xerostomia, like methadone, but also anorexia so the user scarcely eats and becomes severely undernourished. It erodes dental enamel. Want any more? Well it also causes vasoconstriction of the blood vessels which stops any lesions or infections healing. The tooth grinding that is common with crack is another little twist in the dental chaos.

I have not been to a dentist for over twenty years but go and have root canal work which is a deeply unpleasant experience. Three hours of drilling over three sessions. After the talk I find myself driving around Leominster at night looking for a night chemist that will sell me painkillers powerful enough. I am assured that opiates do the trick very effectively.

6/12/05

The Mistletoe sale at Tenbury.

Our mistletoe goes for a lot less than the prices of last week's sale. All a bit of a comedown. We stand around for hours in the drizzly cold and when the sale does happen it is low-key, quick and we somehow never found out who bought it. But it is a sale. It carries the notion of money.

When we were done we went back for a celebratory lunch of bread and cheese and then I went off to Ludlow for more dental work, leaving them to potter in the shards of afternoon light that remained.

06.12.05

Last week we harvested some Mistletoe to sell at Tenbury market so today we went to Tenbury. We sold 4 bunches for £47. This was the first sale from the farm. It has been an all round good experience. Have also fed and looked after the animals.

Andy Pope 2005

The first sale of anything today at Tenbury. A good experience. Katie's done a wonderful record of everything that's happened at the Rock. Andy P, as always, has done the stock work. Andy B had a good conversation with Monty and that's good to see. Keep talking.

Philip

Are we now in profit?!

Rocky

7/12/05

Hard frost that steadily warmed to heavy rain by mid afternoon.

Philip arrived with a trailer packed with eighteen ewes. It is clearly a good thing in itself but I confess I fail to see the romance of sheep. Foul feet, backsides that challenge chickens for horror and complete absence of brain. But the sheep are an important part of the plan and they are all, apparently, pregnant and due to lamb sometime around the beginning of March. All very tame and responding to the rattle of feed in a bucket with manic, square-eyed determination.

So now, despite our boggy, unworkable land, we have chickens, pigs, sheep, garlic and broad beans sown in pots and a hundredweight of garlic unsown in a sack.

This is the very worst time for me. All a struggle.

My garden diary says, in its entirety, 'Dark by 4 p.m. Bed 7.30'.

14/12/05

Today we all had sheep arrive, 18 of them. We place them from the trailer to a temporary field until the fence been done?? The electric fence has been put up and the pig sty is a mess so we put old hay bails down and new bedding down. In myself I feel pissed off. I don't know why? I'm not in the mood to drive the tractor. I would like to do a bit of fencing by myself to do a bit of thinking. We all can do it but we should spread out and do it so it will be quicker.

Andy B

Hi Diary

Today has been exciting. The sheep have come and it's starting to look like a farm. Andy you know why you are pissed off? So speak

to me please. I am a friend you know and when you're feeling
upset so do I. So tell me what's wrong please and cheer up.

Love KT x

14/12/05

Spent the day clearing a patch of rough woodland for David.
Woodland is aggrandising what amounts to a small triangle of
elder in the corner of the field that he had wanted kept back as a
wildlife corner. It is ambiguous and unspoken as to whether this
is under the lease or that we are simply doing it for him as a
favour. Doesn't matter as it is clearly all part of the domain. The
chopping and sawing and dragging to bonfire went well but
wholly incapable of starting the fire. In the end I poured petrol
over it and nearly took all the hair off my head as it lit. Hilarity
all round. Chris intoxicated with the sharp axe – as indeed am I.
Bonded by a blade. Later he and Philip made a stile to get from
the vegetable area into the field without going right round the
outside. Chris is working well, especially when it involves
practical tasks done with one other person. He is by far and
away the most physically competent and independent of them
and slowly his hostility and coldness is thawing.

A new girl came and spent most of the day in the shed with
Kate huddled against the cold. Seems surprisingly normal and
motherly and I find myself reacting with a kind of conventional
middle-England shock when I am told she is a heavy user. Later
Kate says that she is a bad influence and I never see nor hear of
her again.

14/12/05

Not a very good start because we messing around with a fire. I
don't believe in them! And no, I don't want to work on my own. I

do want to work in a group. We should all spread out more and get more done. That way we are all good at different things.

Andy B

Well, I've had a really good day. We made a big fire which took a week to get going. Me and Phillip made a stile and all were very impressed. All is well and happy including Andy B. Hoorahh!!

Chris x

19/12/05

We had our Christmas dinner in the shed at the Rock. A stable. They had said that they would like goose for Christmas so my wife, Sarah, went to huge lengths to find and buy a local one. But they forgot that they had asked for it when it appeared. We also cooked a turkey, which was just as well, and sausages wrapped in bacon – special Kate request. The goose was hugely expensive – about £80 – but staggeringly delicious – easily the best I have had. The shed had a Christmas tree and they had decorated it. The benches were pushed together to make a long table and we had a white tablecloth, some mistletoe and holly. And crackers. I bought them all some presents – lighters, thermal vests etc. – and wrapped them and they all had a kind of party bag/stocking. Tricia cooked lots of veg, Sarah made stuffing, bread sauce and gravy and I bought plenty of wine.

It was fun. Really, really good fun. Philip was there in complete benign, Father Christmas mode and Chris and Kate got gently tiddly and said that it was the best Christmas that they had ever had.

19/12/05

It has been an absolute brill day. We all had a loverly dinner

108

and the goose was phat and I've never tasted such a nice bird. Cheers to Dave and Trish, Monty and Sarah and Rocky and Phill for a fantastic 4 months. Cheers everyone. Katie, Popey and Andy B. My 3 best mates in all the world!
FANTASTIC!!!!

Chris x

PS Yes – just a bit merry!

Hi everyone,

Just a quick thank you 4 today! It was a brill dinner and everyone's merry. Well done everyone. You're my team. My boys.

Love Katie xx

Christmas dinner today. Great day. Feel touched. Monty, Rocky and co. Kate looks like she's having a good time. Really glad I've stayed in Worcester. Happy Christmas.

Andrés 2005

Brilliant!! Nice dinner, really enjoyed it. Hope I'm here next year? The goose was really nice. Monty – nice speech and Kate, Rocky has been wicked. Best friend anyone can make. Phil and Monty and all the group that are eg Andy Breakwell (me), Andrés Pope, Kate, Chris, really nice to work with. Sorry I been childish. Please forgive us. Love you all.

Andy B

PS thanks for your support.

A great day – a great 2005. Bring on 2006!

Rocky

Andy B – don't be sorry mate. We all have to help each other. Love you too mate.

Chris & Popey & Kate & Rocky

It's Christmas at the Rock. Hope everyone has enjoyed the last few months. Wishing everyone a Merry Christmas.

Philip

I then had to spend a week away and did not get back to the Rock until the New Year but the group came a few more days over Christmas just to check up on the animals and to walk around. They added the following to the daybook – Christmas for them was clearly not all good cheer.

28.12.05

Sorry I couldn't come today. I gone to a funeral because my cousin OD. He only just came out of prison (HMP) Glos. Chris Watts his name. Hope you all had a nice time. I did. Sorry for today.
  PS. He was my best friend.

Andy

It has killed me to come today. Had to catch a train at 8.00 am to get to Worcester. My stomach feels rough but least I have come.

Andy P 2005

Me too, yeah yeah

Katie xx

Nice to see Andy and Katie today. I knew they wouldn't miss it. Last time at the Rock in 2005. Happy new year to everyone involved.

Philip

110

January 2006

On 7 January I went and gave a talk to the Soil Association conference about the project. It went down well and many people expressed interest in getting involved. It is, of course, a receptive audience but I was surprised at how this very simple idea catches people's imaginations. I realise that I am in deep and had better keep swimming. There is no turning back.

The group came back in the New Year like a new school term.

03.01.06

Happy New Year

It's bloody cold but apart from that its OK. Did everyone have a good time? I have, hope you all did? I had lots of presents this year, most ever.

Andy B

04.01.06

Hi, it's a new year and a fresh start. I'm not running round for gear no more. I've had enough.

Katie

Feel positive and determined. Going to do my best and think of the bigger picture. I HAVE GOT TO DO THIS.

Andy P 2006

A new year. Everyone seems to have had a good Xmas/New Year and all remains full of hope. Keep it up and best wishes for a successful year to Chris/Andy B/Andy P & Katie – keep firing!

Rocky

09.01.06

Feel a bit unsure of myself.

Andy P

The farm's OK.

Chubby

Chubby is new and is a foursquare, rollicking man in his mid-twenties with a physical presence quite unlike any of the others. This is largely due to the fact that he is not nor ever has been a heroin addict. He was – according to Kate – a heavy amphetamines user and has a very long history of crime, mainly involving car theft. He is not one to back down from physical confrontation either. He has a pronounced limp but is strong and keen to do physical work. Like the others, he will not touch any food that is unknown to him, which excludes almost everything we have to offer beyond bread and bacon.

He is a nice man, with a very straight-forward sense of decency and I get on well with him from the outset. I can see that this last sentence might seem odd following the previous paragraph, but there you are – people are complicated.

Chubby has arrived. Let's see the work shift now!

Rocky

Often reading the daybook was the only way of finding out how they had got on when I was not able to be there. Even then I had to read between the lines.

114

11.01.06

Today feel a bit odd. Everyone is building a pigsty in the barn because the pigs are making a mess. It's this weather because the grass is turned to shit! Damp, wet dirt! I want to do practical because I am a fabricator, metal or wood. I believe we all should spread out because we all don't need to do the same thing. We don't need to hold hands to do things! But I want to thank everyone for being supportive. I don't know why but I want a job because 98% I'm bored. Everyone makes me feel that I'm dumb and thick. I think I woke up on the wrong side of the bed!

Andy B

Why do people have to go home early. We had a really good day today and all worked well. It just makes me feel angry at the end of the day when there is no need.

Katie xx

I'm finding it hard this year. I'm quite pissed off with myself as I have had a bit of a relapse the past week or so. I'm trying to do something about it but where is everyone?

Andy P 2006

(It took me a month to find out what this 'little bit of a relapse' incurred. A crack den, needles and Birmingham were involved.)

We must concentrate on ourselves. Be happy, enjoy the work and remember, we are a team and we must be supportive. We can all get through this!! Come on!!!

Rocky

It's been a good day.

Chubby

Back in November, unbeknown to me, the probation service had arranged, at great expense, for the group to go and work in woods near Wigmore – Wigmore Rolls. Now these are beautiful, ancient woodlands that have been coppiced for charcoal, firewood, hurdles and thatching spars since early medieval times and are potentially fascinating, at least for me. It would involve working with the land, learning about the beauty and intensely sophisticated management of woodland and could connect directly back to the project. But the timing feels wrong. It needs to be sold to them and related directly back to what we are doing at the Rock. It is costing money that could better be spent on the farm. Finally, Wigmore is another half hour on top of a drive that is already too long.

One of the major conceptual differences throughout the first year of the project between myself and some members in the probation services was that they saw the visits to the Rock as away days – a chance to be out in the 'country' and plant some seeds and see animals close-up. Therefore the more varied these days could be the more they might catch the group's interest. It was not an unreasonable view. But it missed the basic premise that I wanted them to own the site, to regard it as a long-term personal project that bonded them closely with it, the produce and the people around it. They did not need entertainment, just encouragement and instruction in order that they might do it themselves.

However the woods were a good place to be and it had been paid for, so they went off for a day, without me, instead of visiting the farm. In truth there was not a lot to do at the Rock in the cold and wet mid-winter and they enjoyed it.

18.01.06

We went coppicing today. I really enjoyed it. Morris was a sound bloke and I think we all enjoyed it. Hard work, but good.

Chris

Hello

Today we went to Wigmore Wood to look at how coppicing was done. Morris the Coppicer showed us how and what to do when chopped and sorted wood was done. It was really interesting and I would like to go again.

Katie xx

Today I cut a branch. No, really, we went coppicing in Wigmore Wood. It was a real eye opener. It was good.

Andy Pope

In the middle of the month there was a suspicion that Andy B had some heroin on him at the Rock. It was only hearsay and never proven or discovered but it was a moment of profound shock for him when he realised that he might well be expelled permanently from the farm even just on suspicion of it being true. As it was he was read the riot act and told that he had no chances left.

22.01.06

Sorry everyone for lying including Rocky & Monty. I really enjoy the feeling as it was true and you Rocky, please forgive us. I promise I tell you the truth from now on. I tell truth whether it hurts. Sorry everyone.

Andy B

Andy, you are already forgiven. All I want you to do is give up HEROIN, enjoy yourself, keep going – you are doing fine.

Rocky

Ex bad boy Chubby woz ere.

Chubby

Popey, Chris, Katie & Andy B all had reviews so we arrived at the farm a bit late today – all the reviews were excellent with new achievable goals set for everyone. I am proud of the achievements you have all made to date and I know how hard you all are trying – thank you.

Rocky

('Reviews' are when they go back to the court which reviews the state of their compliance with the court order. A report is written by their probation officer and the results of their drug testing are included.)

24.01.06

I'm going to have a holiday because I want time away? I need to speak to Sheely to ask can I have 2 weeks of Methadone up front. I might go down Devon to my Auntie's because I want to get out of my town and get away to think things through. Right now I had the best help I ever had and I feel better in myself but I need to make a choice. I don't want to carry on on drugs. I really hate the stuff but it just helps me to cope with things and I try to speak it but its hard to explain. I am not going to take the piss or abuse the system. I either carry on and lose everything or stop and gain my wish.

Wish me luck.

Andy B

25.01.06

Well, today was better for me today as I was in the warm doing the shed. We have moved the old shelf unit and tidied up in here. Everyone seems to be happier in themselves today!!

Monty has popped in today for his dinner but has had to leave early due to some family business. Me and Popey are getting on really well again. Whats going on then with Andy B? He wants a

118

holiday? It will do him the world of good if he goes. I'm off on 14 February for a week to Devon so you will all be on your own.

Love Katie xx

Katie and Andy B off to Devon? Whatever next!!!

Rocky

Neither of them ever did get to Devon or away for any kind of holiday. As none of them have any money, save for drugs, no transport of their own and almost no adult experiences outside crime and drugs, they are not really up to the complications of organising travel, somewhere to stay, money and all the paraphernalia of a holiday. Mind you, nor am I.

Well, I feel today has been very productive. We have all worked extremely hard doing our jobs. All the animals are sorted. The barn has been done, the drain has been completed. Well goodbye and goodnight.

Andy P 2006

Despite the easy, satisfied tone of the above entry Andrés was going through a crisis. He was using again, not speaking to anyone and back into his old habit of eating facing away from the group, staring out the window or falling asleep at the table. It was clear that he was very unhappy. I heard that he was planning to leave and asked him to talk to me about it. He wouldn't talk but promised to stay on. It was very hard to see a man so clearly suffering, but all the evidence is that every addict goes through cycles of getting clean followed by relapse until they finally find a way of staying clean or dying. Or, like a few of the very rich, staying hooked.

Towards the end of the month Andy B admitted that he had a lost weekend. He explained it to me like this:

I went to catch a train home right. But the train was early so I missed it. (Early? Trains are never early. He was late.) And it was another hour for the next train. Then a train came to Birmingham see so I took that (he was intending to go to Evesham – the opposite direction). I met this bloke in Birmingham who offered me some crack, I shouldn't have took it but I did. I had seventy quid's worth. But you see, with crack, you gotta have more so I found I spent 300. It wasn't right but I did it.

Did you use as well?

No. Well only later to calm me down like.

So let's get this straight: on your way home from Worcester to Evesham (a journey of about twenty minutes) you changed your mind, went to Birmingham, spent twenty-four hours and 300 pounds on crack and heroin and didn't get back home until nearly two days later.

That's about it. But you know what? I didn't even enjoy it.

30.01.06

Sorry everyone, I seem to let everyone down and myself because I did the most stupidest weekend I ever did for 1 year and 6 months. Please believe me, it wont happen again. I'm glad I did it because I – to be honest it was SHIT!?
Thank you for your support everyone for when I need you.

Andy

Today feels strange. I feel a bit lost. One of the pigs has hurt their foot and the big chicken has damaged it's eye. I am trying to keep busy and not think of things too much.

Andy P

Well done Popey, keep firing.

Rocky

February 2006

2/2/06

I went straight to Wigmore Rolls to meet the group for a day's coppicing. This is a huge expanse of medieval woodland, dominated by coppiced oak, hazel, ash, field maple, birch and alder, most of which was originally used for charcoal for the iron industry. The ground had a kind of ridge and furrow which was apparently to provide narrow tracks for men, horses and small carts to get the wood out and down to the village below. It was an intensely beautiful place and, for myself, much more exciting than a day at the Rock. However the group arrive uncomfortable, carsick and bored. It would be like getting a cheap flight to a coppice in the middle of icy nowhere. However, the team had been the week earlier and I joined them.

It was bitterly cold – frosty and snowy with a cutting wind – and they were all very late but in itself it was fine and fun. We used axes and chainsaws to clear wood, had a fry-up over a fire and cleaned off the cut wood into firewood, bean sticks and pea sticks. It was not so different from the same scene five hundred years earlier with a gang of motley people hacking into the woods, bundling, huddling against the cold. In itself I loved it.

Chubby got stuck in and chopped with gusto and a new guy, Chris Spires with, unusually for that age group, a tweed flat cap (in the ensuing months I never once saw him without it on) had a real go too. He was just out of prison, released early and had to do the order for the rest of the time of his sentence. I asked him if he was a user and he shook his head. On a script. No need. I'm clean. Kate heard this and rolled her eyes.

Kate and Andrés were lost both to us and themselves. It seems that there is something going on between them and Kate is spending a lot of time at Andrés' flat but it is not bringing much happiness to them. They have no money and were working out how they would get some cigarettes or something to eat in the coming twenty-four hours. I had been to the bank on my way there to get money to buy the sausages, bacon and bread for lunch and had a hundred quid in my pocket. The temptation to lend them a tenner was very great and I put this to Rocky. He told me not under any circumstances. If they spent it on gear and died of an overdose then I would be 'in serious shit. Don't do it.'

6/2/06

After we had all arrived and got ourselves together (they seem to be in a daze when they get out of the car and it takes about half an hour for them to fully unfurl) and had a cup of tea, Rocky stood up and gave a very pointed and heavy-handed talk about the use of drugs and how that if he found anybody using or possessing any drugs on site he would immediately make a citizen's arrest and drive them straight to the nearest custodial police station. No one was above this. There would be no attenuating circumstances. This took me by surprise by its formality and unexpectedness. They listened with due solemnity. Everybody obviously knew more than I did.

There was a new bloke from Leominster. Paul. Tall, fragile. Twenty-six. Lives with his parents, spends hours on his computer and watching cricket on satellite TV. Terrible teeth. Addicted for eleven years. Seems anxious but keen. Keen is good. From Leominster is very good – our first truly local person. Ideally they would either all come from Leominster

February 2006

and the surrounding villages or else we would have a site for them much closer to Worcester. It will happen.

06.02.06

I've really enjoyed my first day and I am excited about what is happening and what is going to happen.

Paul

A welcome to Chris 'Lucky' Spiers and Leominster Paul. I have read your comments and am very pleased to see you have enjoyed yourself today. You both did very well and the group have accepted you, no problems. It was a good day all round for everybody, ploughing, planting, compost digging, animals sorted (the pig is still sick). Tony did something with wire and wood but I don't think it will fly! It was necessary to issue a stern warning to all about Rule No. 1 – NO DRUGS ON SITE. If you know it refers to you – you know the consequences. If not, BEWARE AND DO NOT GET INVOLVED.

Best wishes to you all

Rocky

8/2/06

Went in after a morning's writing to have lunch with them and to specifically talk to Andrés. I got the message that he was thinking of leaving the project. We went and leant over the bars of the new Pig barn and I asked him what the matter was. He rather angrily said that he was not going to talk about it. I said I didn't know what 'it' was. My main concern was that he would stand by me. Not give up – for my sake if nothing else. I didn't know if this

125

was too maudlin and irrelevant but even though I intended it as a heavy-handed ploy I realised I meant it. Anyway he said he would stay and I trust him.

We are at a point where the house could tumble.

So much of this is built upon trust. It is all rather old fashioned. Done on a handshake.

Judging from the daybook Rocky's drug warning has put the cat amongst the pigeons.

08.02.06

Tonight I'm doing some thinking because I thought I had some friends but I always misunderstand. I'm not coming to this farm if everyone is against me and I thought we all stick together, not back stab everyone? If we support each other then yes I will keep coming, if not, I wont bother.

Andy B

13/2/06

Had a phone call from Dee, producer of the TV series, on Friday saying that Andrés had told them (the crew I suppose – this confessional to the camera) that he had found himself in a Birmingham crack-den with a needle sticking into himself without any idea how he had got there. It is sort of funny, sort of glamorous, sort of horrifying but mostly depressing. I suppose this sums up the whole project.

Andrés is in a terrible state. Not speaking, not making eye contact. Lost. As bad as when he first came here.

I had a long talk with Rocky about the state of the group and their drug use. This is actually quite hard as the camera crew follow us everywhere and the deal is that they can film everything and anything on site. But Rocky has certain things that he will not talk about on camera and I do not want to compromise Rocky or place him in an awkward situation.

I think he sees the project as a kind of safe zone for himself where he can relax a little – as long as it is perceived as a success. Failure of any kind is trouble for him – whereas of course it is material for any television documentary!

The future of the project and its funding – in probation or police terms – depends upon measurable success. Rocky often tells me to be patient, that success must be judged on their terms not ours – but has also hinted that his employers do not always share that view. He constantly treads a fine line and it must be exhausting.

We spent the day clearing the ditch alongside the field – almost a pond rather than a ditch and cutting back the hedge before laying it. As a result of the general discontent of going all the way to Wigmore Rolls, Maurice the woodman with the bowler hat says that he will come to us once a week, so he was instructing them.

Some of them, the Chrises and Chubbys of the world, like this kind of background, housekeeping work of hedging, ditching, fencing and the like. It is vigorous and project-based and they can see what is to be done and what they have achieved at the end of it. Others, like Kate and Andrés, see it as a distraction from the real thing. Kate resents the fact that David will benefit from it after we have gone. She suspects it to be a ploy to get slave labour to do his dirty work. I try and explain that good husbandry is about caring for all the landscape and investing in the future but know as I do so that she thinks I am a twat for saying it. This could be because she tells me precisely that. But her daybook entry tells another version of the day altogether:

13.02.06

I feel really motivated today which has not happened in a long time. If anybody here needs help or anyone to talk to please do so. I am trying my hardest to stay clean and I need you all to help me as I'm finding it difficult at the moment. Everyone is starting to work really well as a team so keep the good work up lads.

Love Katie

14.02.06

To the group! There are many people here who are having problems. Seeing past their drug use. I know just as much as any of you that it's sometimes easier to use a bag of gear or to get on that glass dick and get off your face than to face up to your problem or try and be drug free but beyond all that pain of withdrawal and urges and cravings. We have all got the motivation and determination to get drug free or else none of us would be here at the farm. We have more support from Probation, Rocky, Toni, Jack and Phil and Monty that we should be able to talk about our problems, than hide them away. We should all help, support and respect each other's views and beliefs, right or wrong. I am trying to be drug free and maintain on my script at the moment. So please support me as much as possible. I will be as supportive as I can to all of you who need to talk and want help. I hope you take this seriously and give it all you can. You are all thought of as valuable members of the group and all needed at the farm. I also know you're going to find things hard. Just remember things could only get better and there is always someone more worse off than ourselves! Please stay positive. A lot of people and friends have put time and effort, energy and also suffered abuse. We know where we went wrong in our lives and we are trying to correct it! Anyway, enough said. Just remember who gave us this chance to be here!!

Love KTxxxx

15/2/06

Sarah's Birthday so I do not go over to the project. We go shopping, have lunch with friends and go to the Black Mountains for thirty precious minutes – quick battery charge – before picking the children up from the bus at five. The longest we have spent together for many months.

At the farm the crisis between Andrés and Kate must have reached some kind of head judging from the daybook (Andrés often signs his name as Andy in the daybook):

15.02.06

Sorry Katie about Monday night. Today hope I can work but on my own if I can because if we spread out we get more jobs done.

So bye then – Andy

PS – have a fair day if not good or sort of in between. So hope you all had better. Thank you.

MEETING HELD ON DRUGS MENACE

Hereford Times, *Thursday 16 February, 2006*

The menace of drugs and drug dealers in the community will come under the spotlight at Leominster public meeting.

The town council is organising 'Keeping Leominster A Safe Place To Live' – a discussion forum with speakers from police, the local drugs advice service and other bodies.

Mayor Roger Hunt said the meeting, on February 21, was being organised after a group of residents at

129

last year's annual town meeting voiced fears over dealers on their doorstep.

Since then there had been a police crackdown. A number of dealers had been dealt with and the situation in Leominster was certainly no worse than many other towns.

'But we can't rest on our laurels,' said Mr Hunt. 'Continued vigilance over drugs is essential.'

20/2/06

I am constantly assaulted by the thought that I am an impostor and only toying with this whole scheme. Not really involved enough. But that is balanced by the equally teryifying thought that I am right in it – up to the neck – and equally inadequate.

Cold day, east wind, rain, hail, but sun too.

I went late today – Howard Sooley here from nine to photograph the garden for the *Observer*. Felt exhausted – almost ill with weariness so had to really stiffen the sinews before going. I always dread it – it feels like an examination and an arduous, bleak one at that. But I got there about twelvish. Rocky immediately collared me and said that we needed to come up with some action – they had all had enough of digging trenches and cutting down trees. We need to plant and sow and restore the focus on what it was all about.

It is, of course, *all* about ditches and hedges and caring for the landscape. But this is a view they find hard to understand. Rocky was – is – worried at losing their interest. His mantra as a measure of success is – 'they are here'. Meaning that they have to make a number of positive decisions and actions in a wholly chaotic life to actually get themselves here.

He said that it was essential that I show the same enthusiasm there – at the Rock – that I did when I gave the talk to the probation service at Ludlow last spring. That I must match the way I spoke about it with my actions at the farm. He is right of course. My role is to enthuse and inspire. I find this difficult when I have to organise too. But I must try.

After lunch I went off and had a chat with Chris Davies, Andrés and Kate and Rocky in the tunnel. And the film crew of course. It is a kind of extra privacy to have the crew in a secluded place. Kate said how much she hated the digging and 'tree-chopping'. The other two said that they were happy and not alarmed. Andrés – who has been using a lot of crack and heroin recently – was much better and more positive. Saw the bigger picture. Chris wanted to work to get a job. Kate said she was fucking bored. Bored of all the mud and digging.

I want to plant plants and sow seeds. Can't we sow stuff *now*?

It was like a child wanting to go and play or buy sweeties. I talked about the desire to make the land good, to invest ourselves into somebody else's future. Also the need to push forward.

Rocky very keen that we react to the birdflu situation. David offered part of the outshut to the Dutch barn (where the pigs are for the moment and where, when they have gone tomorrow, we must get ready for the sheep to come in to lamb) so we may have to fix that up very soon. I am not convinced by the birdflu scare. Everyone loves a good scare, be it newspapers, government or Health and Safety execs. But there are far greater dangers at every turn of the unremarkable day.

Tomorrow the two boars and the gilt with the damaged leg go off to the butcher, Griffith's at Leintwardine, some ten miles up the road right on the border between Shropshire and Here-fordshire. We made plans for moving the remaining gilt. She is to remain with us until she comes into season, when we will take her to Ray who has a boar. Then she can come back to us pregnant and we will rear her offspring. Having had piglets she

131

will then become a sow. Philip anxious about taking them – asked where Griffith's were – aggressive about birdflu, saying that all the birds would have to be destroyed anyway so no point in protecting them.

Used my chainsaw to help cut back the trees and hedge along the ditch but did very little actual work with them today.

Left in bright sunshine feeling positive, enthused and inspired. I have to give it the time it needs. The only problem remains that this is more than the time that I have.

21/2/06

Pigs went to butcher today. I rang before they got there to discuss size of joints and type of sausages. We are having 50 per cent pork, 25 per cent Shropshire sizzlers and 25 per cent pork and leek. The sizzlers have, I believe, blue cheese to thank for that extra bit of sizzle. The butcher said that the joints and sausages would be ready for collection on Friday. I immediately thought bugger, I don't really have time to get them, but agreed.

21.02.06

Pigs gone to slaughter but nobody has written anything! Thoughts please. I'm sad.

Rocky

22/2/06

Went into Leominster early to buy a deep freeze to take the pork. (Also bought some Gloucester Old Spot bacon so that they could see the type of thing that they would be getting. Three-quarters fat and the meat a slightly pink brown.) Anyway, went into electric shop, asked for the biggest freezer they had, saw it and said I would take it. It was £395. I had the Land Rover outside so asked for help loading it up. The owner said that it was better to transport it upright (it is an upright type) and he would be happy to do that for me. OK. It would come a little later in the morning. When I went to sign the chit the bill read £415. I said that I thought it was £395? Yes he said but delivery is £20. But you offered to deliver it for me. You didn't say that you would charge for doing so – and certainly didn't offer me the choice of accepting that charge.

Oh we always charge £20 for delivery. But it's free in town mind.

I rejected the offer, and there followed much palaver trying to change the card. In the end he handed me a £20 note and I went off to move the Land Rover just a little closer. But I then realised that it would not fit. So I had to go back to the shop, hand back his twenty quid, apologise profusely in an awkwardly jokey way and drive away. Humiliation all round.

When I got to the Rock no one was there. It was bitter with a bleak, cutting wind. The sheep implored and followed me through the fence and the one remaining pig had ears lifted by the wind and a slightly porcine air of despair. When they arrived (Chubby, Chris Spires, Kate, Andrés, Andy B, and Paul; Rocky and Tony drove them) Kate and Chubby prepared the place for the freezer and cleaned out the shed. Andy B was reluctant to go outside and work but I bullied him to and he complained that he didn't like working in groups so I set him up with a bonfire which he and Tony fed all day, clearing the ditch in the process.

The rest of us cleared a space for the pig by moving a trailer load of rubbishy wood (which Andy B burnt) and four trailers of compost which we shovelled and piled up next to the other compost heaps. This was good work because it kept us warm on what was the coldest day we have had there so far.

133

Andrés still up and buoyant and told me that he had bought a bag of heroin the other day (this is actually a little sack made from a cigarette paper containing perhaps quarter of a teaspoonful of powder and looking like the salt in old crisps packets) and threw it away. He said that if he had a chance to get away – to work for Amnesty International or on a farm well away from Worcester – he would go cold turkey on methadone – tell his mother to lock him in a bedroom. Paul, the tall, melancholy lad from Leominster agreed. 'I wouldn't wish it on my worst enemy.' Paul's front teeth are fascinatingly stained and worn.

I ask Chris Spires, the new bloke, to come and sit with us at the table at lunch. No, he says, I'm a Billy, me.

What's a Billy?

Billy-no-mates someone else says.

Chris is defiantly uncooperative, avoiding any and every way of joining in the group. But like a child, you can see that he wants to and never wholly alienates himself.

Chubby won't eat any of the food on offer. So far he has only eaten fried egg rolls in the four weeks he has been with us. I ask him what's wrong with the chicken.

It's got bones Mont.

Bones?

Can't touch nothing with bones. He shakes his head. No way. No bones at all Mont. You ask my mum.

I notice that Andrés eats something which is an improvement on the past few weeks. Paul makes me a cup of tea. This is an important act of friendship. It is very milky and I hate milky tea. I drink it all.

After lunch we move the pigs' ark which is embedded in mud and full of straw. We take it in turns to shovel this straw out kneeling in the ark on six weeks' worth of bedding from four pigs. It should be disgusting but it is the first warm place all day. When we lift the ark a rabbit pops out and scuttles off across the fields. In its new position on the concrete and with hurdles and fences all ready we go to move the pig. In the past they have followed a bucket with food in it obsessively. This time she takes off across the field and for half an hour we chase her, trying to lasso her and grab her ears. She squeals with anger but does not try and go far. All she really wants is to trot around a bit having been cooped up indoors for four weeks. In the end we (all ten of us plus David with the crew in hysterics trying not to laugh too much as they film) gently herd her into her new home.

I leave early, satisfied that it is done. Odd to get home with plenty of daylight. But it was a good day, positive and full of energy and – hurrah – some laughter.

22.02.06

Not a bad day, did fire only with Tony. It's been a bloody cold day very bloody cold but fire kept me warm.

Andy

It has been very productive today. Moved the single lone pig to a new home. Cleaned out the barn and everyone worked as a team and got on. It has been good. Feel really positive.

Andy P

God [*sic*] day, (bit cold tho)

Chubby

24/2/06

Nothing much happens. It is cold. We are playing at farming.

600 pounds worth of seeds are ordered. If a fraction of this germinates we have tons – literally – of vegetables to sell. This lot won't manage it. I can't believe it will happen.

Christ.

I ring Philip to check that he has collected the pork from the butcher. He has and it just – only just – fits in the freezer.

25/2/06

Important that it is called the Rock. Steady. Permanent. Safe.
Run by Rocky.

Lay awake much of the night thinking about failure. Got up at five and listened to music whilst trying to sort this out. Nothing to sort of course. What is needed is a kind of rhythmic, steady structure that everyone involved can tap into. I cannot do that. It is not for want of desire but lack of ability. Can't make the beat.

I realise that the management situation is a real problem. We need the horticultural/agricultural equivalent of Rocky who operates from the base. Philip lives forty minutes away and has his contracting that is clearly still important to him. We need someone living there, working seven days a week. who is entirely proactive and prides themselves on running it like a ship. Who lives and breathes it. All I have to do is to decide *what* we do.

27/2/06

Bad day. We all agreed that there was an air of hollowness about. It was tangible – if an absence can be held. I was very tired – even ill – and pushed myself to go. It was to be a hedgelaying day but Maurice and the hedgelayer Ron (whom I greeted with: I gather you are Ray. Sort of, he replied. But Ron is better) did not turn up till twelve and then David took them off across the fields to show them the kind of hedgelaying he wanted. Welsh style said Ron (Ray) dismissively. I can do that of course. But if you want

136

to win any competitions you got to do Midlands style. Anyway he was persuaded to do Welsh style – which involves a bushier content, the use of some 'dead' wood and few stakes all set at angles and not straight. Paul and Andrés set to with enthusiasm and stuck with it all day.

Laying hedges is certainly not a skill that every farmer acquires although I saw a hedge at Monkland that Philip had done quite beautifully. But some people have a feel for it and although it was a rare and rather arcane country craft in my Hampshire youth in the 60s and 70s, it is now done a great deal in this part of the world, encouraged by good subsidies and grants.

It involves thinning back all the sides of an overgrown hedge and then cutting back the upright stems so that they are held together by just a sliver of bark and wood and carefully folded down at forty-five degrees. Stakes are driven in every yard or so all along the hedge and the folded – but still living – growth woven between them. The 'Welsh style' involves using some of the brash cut to make the hedge thinner to bulk it out and fill gaps. Midland style is leaner and less bulky. But all laid hedges aim at a solid barrier that, before barbed wire, could keep stock in or out; because there is still an unbroken line of bark and cambium running down the stem to the root, the hedge will burst into life in spring, throwing up strong upright shoots which will provide the material to be laid when it is done again in some twenty years or so.

Kate and Chubby would not go outside so I set them up carving spoons, with Kate cutting herself almost immediately. It feels like the soft option – not even therapy really; although Kate tells me she has to have an operation on her stomach. Why? Because being sick has damaged all her stomach muscles (meaning her oesophagus I think).

Why are you sick? Is it the heroin?

I dunno really. It's not smack – that just stops the pain.

So what causes it? Is it crack?

Crack makes you sick, yeah. If you're greedy it makes you puke.

So why do it? If it makes you sick and ruins your stomach why smoke the stuff?

It's the buzz. Three mins of buzz and then you throw up. Then you do it again.

Some statistics from the New English and Welsh Arrestee Drug Abuse Monitoring (NEW-ADAM) programme:*

- 69 per cent of all arrestees tested positive for one or more illegal drugs.
- 38 per cent tested positive for opiates and/or cocaine (including crack).
- Arrestees using opiates and crack in the last 12 months represented just one tenth of those interviewed but accounted for nearly one third (31 per cent) of illegal income reported. On average these users accounted for an illegal income of £24,000 per year.
- 89 per cent of arrestees who committed one or more acquisitive crimes and had used heroin and crack cocaine acknowledged a link between their drug use and offending behaviour. (*One can only assume that the other 11 per cent were thick or deluding themselves.*)

*

I parked my Land Rover and Chris S leant over it.

Cost a lot them extended chainsaws don't they.

Yup.

Get a hundred quid for them I do. Hold their value well.

What about normal chainsaws?

* Taken from 3,091 arrestees at 16 sites in a two-year period.

Only get about thirty quid. I once had a van-load mind. About twenty of them. That was a good night.

Where you get them from?

Sheds, work sites and places. Vans like yours. Do you feel more worried now you mix with people like us?

Nope, but I watch where I park it a bit more.

You should. Parked car is good. Bosh, nip in and it's gone. I once nicked a grinder when I pulled up at traffic lights. It was just sitting there on the road so I leant out and had it. They chased me down the road which was a laugh.

Lunch was our own leg of Tamworth pork with roast potatoes, apple sauce, carrots and gravy. It should have been a triumphant celebration but they were mostly utterly unimpressed. The pork was superb – really delicious – but they showed no awareness or sense of occasion. Three of them refused to sit at the table or taste the meat.

Before we went home I spoke to them about this, asked them what they thought of eating their own pig. Only Andrés said that it was important and significant. The others sniggered or just didn't know what I was talking about. I pushed them and said I regarded it an important – *really* important moment, deeply symbolic moment – to be eating our own beast that we had reared.

It's a pig Monty, Chris Davies said. We got them to make meat and now it's being eaten. Job done.

I said that we should share some between us, keep a lot for eating ourselves and also for an open day but share some now to take home. They all wanted as much as possible, treating it like a freebie – not as their own – our – capital. Chris S tried to nick some – when challenged, he said There's loads there. It was obvious that he had no concept of it as communal property. Others wanted the biggest pieces possible – even though they had had nothing to do with the pigs or didn't eat any at lunch.

I was furious with them. As angry as I have ever been with

139

them. I realised that none of it had any meaning to them at all. This was just a day out that fulfilled a court order.

Philip and I talked about this after they had gone. He was disgusted with them, said that they had gone backwards and that we should be stricter. I think that from now on we will start each day with a meeting round the table to talk about the day's work, who is going to do what and what we expect to achieve. Also rotas for everyone so that the basics are covered and responsibility shared. Also reinforce lunch rule: everyone has to sit at table and share food. If they don't like it they don't eat it. Only alternative our own produce but this is the exception not the rule. The point is to share food and eat it together. No food or drink brought onto site. None.

Important to stress that this is not like anything else they have ever done. This is different. If they don't want to do it then they can go. No one should be there that does not want to.

Rocky's agenda is to get them there – what they do when there is always better for him than the alternative. This will not do. I must be tougher with him.

Left with overwhelming sense of disappointment, anger and weariness. Fucking ungrateful pieces of shit.

27.02.06

Today has been really good. Feel good inside myself. Have help and learned to do an old fashioned farm fence. Hope to feel as positive as this tomorrow.

Andy P

Today has probably been the best day on the farm for me so far because we did the hedge laying and I really enjoyed doing it and am looking forward to carrying on doing it next Monday.

Paul

Today has been fair. I had worse. Monty moaned about pig's
gone – he must of loved them!! Sorry Monty! Thanks for today.

Andy B

Good day, bad day.

Chris

WORD OF THE WEEK – HONESTY

28/2/06 5.30 a.m.

Woke about four going over this. No point in obsessing about it
but I do need to get a grip of the situation.

I see that one of the problems is if they treat the project just
like another of Rocky's days out. The principle behind those is
that as long as they turn up, do not use drugs or break the law,
then whatever they do, say or contribute is better than the
alternative. I want more than that.

Tomorrow I will institute these changes.

1) When they arrive, quick drink and then we all sit round
   the table to discuss what we are going to do, how we
   will do it, why, and who.
2) From now on we shall have rotas for Jankers, the
   chickens, sheep, pigs, and watering.
3) Back to insisting on the food rules – which are:
   • No food or drink brought onto site.
   • We all share the same meal, eaten at a table.
   • The only alternatives to this are our own products –
     i.e. eggs, sausages and in a few weeks, bacon. This to
     be eaten at the table with everyone else. I don't want
     Rocky running a café.

141

- No ad hoc breaks. We have a drink when they arrive, there is lunch and a drink before they leave. That's it.
4) We finish each day with a cup of tea and, sitting round the table, discuss what we have done and anything that we want to say.

These three assemblies are important and all about sharing, equality and commitment.

I want commitment, hard work, interest and a real desire to make the project work for them as individuals and us as a team. If they are genuinely not interested then I don't want them there. It is not punishment but a chance to do something that they can be proud of, to get off gear and open up the possibilities of work and staying off the godawful stuff.

This morning Rocky sent me this email:

Dear Monty,

I, like you, think of something that might instil some group enthusiasm in a deep and meaningful conversation and then find that it all falls on stony ground, with regard to the two points you tried to cover last thing yesterday one the demise of the pigs I spoke to Popey, Katie and Chubby on the return journey and their comments were along the lines that you suggested with regard to the drug usage effectively they say they have had so much going on in their lives which have caused them serious problems that they have no room to be sentimental about what is the natural end to rearing animals for food maybe it is you and me who are too soft. !!!!!!! secondly it was an important day yesterday when we ate something we produced for the first time, not withstanding the eggs but their response was that they see every day on the farm as good positive and constructive with the odd varying change so they could not separate out eating the pork as a special day.

It is very difficult to know how to treat them as a group or more importantly as individuals it may seem that you and I have been in their lives for a long time i.e. six months but if you reduce it to hours it is only about 150 max so our influence will take a long time to bear fruit, but I hope you agree that things with all of them are improving their stamina in actually returning to the farm is amazing concerning the length of the journey and some of the boring and mundane work necessary however that we have been doing recently. The police continue to be supportive of the project and it is clear the offending pattern of the majority of the offenders has ceased or reduced tremendously, their drug dependency is also falling I hope one day soon to have something like 5–6 of them giving negative tests. I, like you, also get frustrated with them and sometimes wonder where we are going but we have taken on this project with hope in our hearts and faith in humans to change so sometimes what they need is a gentle arm around the shoulder and constant encouragement they have enough people shooting them down we must always try and boost their self esteem and make them believe that we believe in them and anyway when the sun shines we will all feel much better.

Hope to see you Wednesday
Rocky

March 2006

1/3/06

I instituted all my changes this morning. It was clearly a shock to them. They feel shaken out of their comfort zone and don't really like it. Rocky must have said something to them on the way over because as soon as they arrived Andrés asked to speak to me and said that they did appreciate everything here. Everything they saw was a measure of what they had achieved. The shed. The tunnel. The animals. The ditches and hedges. They were all signs and symbols of success. He was anxious and almost pleading.

Then Rocky took me to one side and in a roundabout way asked me not to lay into them. He said that he knew that it was hard – but that there were many pressures from the probation service for this to fail (what pressures? Why?) and we must not be seen to fail at all. The long and the short of it is that Rocky is scared of any kind of failure because it would be a chance for his critics in the probation service to jump on him. He doesn't want this to happen because he believes in them, his work and in the project. He doesn't want me to blow it.

Anyway only Chris Davies and Kate reacted badly (Chris Spires was not there – which was a pity). Chris said:

I think you have ruined everything. It was all great before. You are just making it all rules and ruined.

Kate said It's like fucking prison, rules and fucking regulations. I'm not going to be fucking spoken to like this – and stormed out, slipping and tripping on the mud and ice. She had hardly communicated for the rest of the day and spent the afternoon sitting in Rocky's car. She has been using very heavily and looks awful.

Andy B got up in the middle and made himself a cup of tea. I challenged this – pointed out that the lack of focus and engagement was part of the problem. So he v-e-r-y slowly made the tea – like a seven year old – and sat down again with what can only be described as a smirk.

David spoke to them about what he was being paid in rent (£200 per month) and that any tenant would be expected to look after fences, hedges, drains etc. In other words they were not working 'for' him – just looking after their tenancy. Anyway, the air was cleared.

Afterwards Chris Davies said the thing that troubled him was being paired with Kate for the rotas. He knew he couldn't do it with her. I told him to give it a go and see how it worked. The truth is that none of them want to do anything that is uncomfortable. The worst of them refuse to try or give up within minutes in an uncongenial situation. The best of them barely tolerate it. I don't know to what extent this is the particular junkie culture or just modern youth.

I think that the symbol of muddy, wet graft is important. It is so at odds with most modern street life with its soft hands and white trainers and trousers. I sound like some dreadful old codger. I am one. But I know that this lot can do it. They are just as resourceful and tough as their grandfathers that fought wars, ploughed fields with horses and went down mines. It just needs tapping into.

01.03.06

Today has been sound. Have moved the sheep (well, moved the fence in the barn). Cleaned the big barn. Have been told some ground rules thanks to Rock, Monty, Philip and the rest of the team.

Andy P

A day for reflection – all of us.

Rocky

3/3/06

Got there early to have a meeting with Philip. The probation service has not offered to renew his contract on 31 March on its present terms but to reduce him to part-time or finish the arrangement altogether. He is confused as to how it could be done part-time and says that he would have to charge almost as much as full time to 'make it work'. He is a thoughtful, intelligent and kind man and very good with the group. But it worries me how clear his grip is on the minutiae of vegetable growing, let alone doing so organically and within a contract that is limited to less than forty hours a week and with him living so far away. It is not ideal for him or us.

We had a good day's work, finishing clearing the ditch/pond. Only four came – Kate, Andrés, Chubby and Paul – and they all remained busy all day on a rotation of hedgelaying, clearing and working a pole lathe that Maurice the greenwood man set up for us.

For the first time everyone ate everything at lunch. It was veg soup and ham rolls. No complaints, no discussion about how it might be different in any way, no leaving a scrap. A triumph.

7/3/06

A week's holiday at home. Felt unwell and typically, didn't know what to do with myself but furious when asked to come in filming. Rule number one with any TV company – if you are officially on holiday never, ever tell them where you will be. Rained all day so couldn't garden. The Demeter seeds (all grown biodynamically and from Botton which is just a few miles away from where Sarah and I lived for a year high up on the North York Moors back in 1979) arrived and I sorted them all. They seem inadequate – tiny packets for such a big field – but there are many different varieties and it has cost nearly 600 quid.

13/3/06

Took the seeds in and explained them all, laid them out on the table (extra table had arrived). Most showed genuine interest – except Andy B. The truth is that most have what would broadly be termed as 'mental problems' and therefore are, by definition, odd. But then I too have 'mental problems' so feel at home with that.

It was a very cold, muddy day and a bit grim. It has felt like a long winter and spring is nowhere in sight.

13.03.06

Well this is my first entry since 08.02. and a lot has happened since then. Last week me and Paul started to make a new pig pen. Also an incident occurred which 3 of the team has had a stern talking to. I won't mention any names but they know who they are.

Today I put a new latch on the barn door which will help to keep the door shut. Monty is going on about some seeds and it's not very interesting to me. The sheep are expected to give birth today but then again, people have been saying that for weeks. Anyway, all is well and I'm feeling fine. Oh, and the pork was very tasty indeed!

Chris

But at lunch the first lamb was born. Kate, Andrés and Paul immediately went off to watch and help. Philip was in his element, steering and guiding them. Kate, the most fastidious of people who will not eat anything on a plate if one aspect of it is, in her eyes, contaminated, delivered a lamb without any qualms, wiping the afterbirth off with straw and clearing its mouth of mucus. She christened it Eric. Three more followed throughout the afternoon. This is a really big moment for us for every obvious reason. We have bought piglets, raised, killed and eaten them, sowed seeds and seen them appear (eventually) through the surface of the soil, and now we have watched and helped sheep give birth. It is all entirely natural and normal but so remote from most people's lives.

In the afternoon I sowed some seeds in the solar tunnel with Kate, Chubby and Chris Spires (both playing around in an irritating way – makes me feel like an inept schoolmaster trying to keep order. I have no interest in this at all). This is a bit of a token act to fufil the general desire to sow stuff and move forward rather than a considered piece of horticultural timing as I cannot see much germinating in this cold.

Had a very shit day. Bit better after dinner. Getting better? Sorry the way I behave.

Andy B

Today has been very eventful. Two lambs have been born and Katie helped deliver the second one. It was a great experience

151

to watch. We started the first major sowing of seeds. Today has been good.

Andy P

Thanks to Philip for letting me deliver my first lamb!! Which is a boy and a girl was delivered first. I was really excited to have to pull her out. Sorry if I have been miserable lately.

Katie

Andy B – do not keep beating yourself up! You are doing OK. Just keep going and please realize you can rely on others if you need help.

Katie. Cheer up. Be strong, be proud of what you have achieved to date. You are proving a lot of people wrong – DO NOT GIVE UP!!!!

Chris S – hope you are enjoying yourself and get your script sorted. Keep helping others – PS – MONTY IS **NOT** A TOSSER. He is trying to understand all your problems. Help him to keep in touch with your thoughts!

Best wishes to you all.

Rocky

I spoke to Rocky about his life. Rocky – heroic, wise, sane man that he is – has a particular ironic, slightly quizzical tone of voice that doesn't really come off the page. Our relationship is one that has developed into disrespectful banter, like men do, but if he admires me a quarter as much as I admire him then I am doing OK.

Rocky Hudson

How old am I? Well I was I was born in 1952. In Ross on Wye in Herefordshire. I was brought up at Brockhampton, about five miles north of Ross and went to school in Ross. My father was a farmworker and gamekeeper. I have two brothers, one works on a farm and the other is a gamekeeper on the same estate in Herefordshire.

When I was seventeen I left and became a police cadet and joined the force in 1971. I did three years on the beat and then joined the CID in Worcester. I was posted to Malvern in 1974 and stayed there till 1987 when I joined the drugs squad which was based in Worcester and Upton on Severn. I was a detective constable. I never really tried to pass the exam. Poor old Ange wanted me to pull my finger out. But I was enjoying the job.

I got married to Ange on 21 May 1974. She came from Malvern. Best day's work I ever did.

I was always catching druggies in Malvern and when the chance came up I decided to join the drugs squad. It was a change of environment. A challenge. In 1987 heroin was around but a small group that were well-known to the police. There was a bit of LSD and amphetamine sulphate but cannabis mainly and cannabis plants. Plants are good because they can't be swallowed when you kick the door down . . .

There were heroin deaths in and around Malvern at that time. It was quite a busy centre for heroin and it was definitely a growing problem. There wasn't a great deal of criminality to support it but we became aware that if things didn't get sorted then the country would face a drugs explosion. Which is what has happened.

Even in those early days the drugs squad seemed to convince the powers that be in the police that it was going to become a bigger problem. So not enough was done about it.

But I remember when crack was becoming a major problem in

153

the States in the early 90s and there were dire warnings that it would come over here and we would be swamped with it. But it never happened like that. The crack problem crept up gradually. Now of course it is a major problem.

After the drug squad I went into drug intelligence work, based in Worcester. Then I was monitoring sex offenders alongside the probation service. That was rewarding work.

I retired in February 2002 by which time the situation was chaotic. Heroin just exploded in the 1990s.

Heroin has steadily been on the increase all the time. Heroin dealers are business people. It's all about money. And like all competent business people they make sure that they sell it or they create a market where they can sell it.

It has created a lost generation of kids who get involved and it is very difficult to move away from it. They are all stuck at the age that they first got involved, so life experiences stop at that age. They are stuck in that box.

What we are doing here is showing them that there is life outside that box.

They haven't got the skills to go out and get themselves jobs or to maintain a job if they do manage to find one. It can be quite scary for them out there. So they poke their heads out and then go back inside the box where it is safe. In their own world they are people but if they come and join us they carry the stigma of being drug users, thieves etc. In our world they feel insignificant and unworthy. They can't do it.

Perhaps we – you and I – expect too much of them.

The truth is that we are putting them in a position where they are likely to fail. I worry that there is a danger that we are pushing them too fast. Look at all of them – all over 8–10 years into the drug experience and we are trying to get them out of that in six months.

There are times when I have been very angry. When we aren't doing enough to protect kids getting into situations, who go wrong and continue to go wrong. We – as a society – are not doing enough to stop this situation developing.

We are talking about Herefordshire here – an idyllic area, a nice place to live. We are inundated and can't handle it. People are being stabbed to death and cut up for the drugs hidden in their bodies. Just imagine what it must be like in big cities like Manchester and London.

It's no longer a game.

When I retired I originally became civilian assistant to my replacement but I had to be interviewed for the job along with about eight other applicants. So if I had failed the interview I wouldn't have been good enough to help myself!

Then I was offered the opportunity to work with drug users jointly with the police, probation and health. I named the project the Elgar project. It was designed to change prolific priority offenders. I would monitor them, do a lot of sport with them, picked them up and made sure that they attended appointments, making sure that their health was sorted out. I sorted out their court situation and made sure that they didn't breach their orders. I was with them eight hours a day. I got their families involved and met their mums, dads and girlfriends. I became a human tag.

The probation service is overloaded with numbers that they are expected to supervise and this puts them in an impossible situation. They cannot physically find the time to spend with their clients. So I decided that ten was the max that I could have at any time for the scheme to succeed. This meant more time with fewer people.

My budget was my wages plus a car, a phone and about £2000 in expenses. I would meet them for breakfast at Tesco's. I knew you wouldn't approve of that. But they didn't eat otherwise.

The Elgar project was a resounding success and lasted for fourteen months and then this project came along. So this project totally destroyed the Elgar project! I got into this because I volunteered to help Hereford one day a week – so I could keep the Elgar project going. Look what one day a week has led to! I knew you'd be trouble.

I get into Worcester police station at eight and check to see if anyone has been arrested overnight. Then I organize Jack and Tony. When we started I had no help at all. I don't know how I did it. I go round ringing them all and picking them up. We have to get to the chemist with each of them to get their scripts plus any little jobs they need doing, trying to get as many as we can here for as close to 10.30 as possible. Kate is always the best. Always ready as soon as I arrive. Always has to have the front seat. Martin used to always have the front seat. It would have been interesting to have had them two together . . .

I've got pressure from the police to introduce more thieves and fewer heroin addicts into the scheme. More prolific offenders. But real prolific offenders don't get caught. Kate is probably the most prolific offender in Worcester. When she's using all the shares plummet in the stores.

What does the future hold? Well some days I get so pissed off I just want to throw the towel in. I get demoralised, dejected, defeated, depressed – but it's because I expect so many positive results that are for me rather than the individuals.

But you have to think how far they have come. We have to work within the constraints of the order but we shouldn't be thinking about those sort of time restraints. It means that if they haven't sorted themselves out by the end of their order they are left high and dry.

It is a job that is going to be difficult to leave. No matter when you leave you will be abandoning somebody. There is a sign up in the police station saying 'I opened myself to you and then you left'. There will never be a good time to leave.

14/3/06

The Steering Group meetings were due to happen once a month but I had only been to one so far, either because I was committed elsewhere or because I knew that there was absolutely nothing to report and that this nothing would take up much time that would be expertly handled by David Reeve and the probation service. However I went along this evening and Katie and Andrés came too. Andrés stood up and spoke strongly and well about what we were doing and how positive it all was. This was the first time that any of them had had a chance to speak to the group or anyone from the local community. I was proud of him. We spoke about an open day with 31 May as a possible date. All present impressed and supportive.

Tomorrow filming for 'Gardeners' World' starts and everything changes – that sucks in my time in an unnegotiable, monolithic way. On the project, despite the presence of the film crew, I am not a 'presenter'. I am the runner, researcher and one of the team. No concessions or privilages. At GW I am collected by car and receive a degree of conventional TV presenter deference – tempered, thank God, by plenty of earthy humanity and also the control of a geared-up production team. Not a lot of room for movement once we get filming.

Whilst I was filming Kate got the results of her last few drug tests, which were clean. Triumph all round and she rang to tell me. Even Chubby was moved to write more than a sentence in the daybook.

15.03.06

Fair play Katie for getting your cleans in! Keep it up!!

Chubby

Today I got my negative results so thanks for the support Chubby, Rocky n the rest of the team. Today the shed has

been cleaned by Chubby n me. Please keep it clean n respect it
as we have to get ready 4 open day.

Thanx, Katie

Fairplay everyone, had a fair day.

Andy B

20/3/06

Another bitterly cold, raw day. The vernal equinox tomorrow
and spring seems a long way away from the Rock. I dreaded
going in – everything I was heading towards seemed to be a
problem that I had no desire to solve. There was a long email
from Tricia waiting for me when I got up expressing unhappiness with the food set-up. She feels unappreciated and stretched
to provide the sort of meals that she has been asked to make,
given the resources available. This, in itself, is not a food
problem – we can easily sort out alternative arrangements
now that we have our own ham, eggs, bacon, sausages and
pork. All I have to do is buy some cheese, pickle, bread and fruit
and we have good food that we can supplement with home-
made soup. I suspect that it is a symptom of an underlying
feeling about what she and David are giving to the project
without due appreciation.

As it turned out we only had Andrés, Chubby, Chris Davies
and Paul here as Kate was ill, Chris Spires awol and Andy B at
the job centre. Paul was irritable and morose because he has
given up cannabis (or, I suspect, cut back) after being found with
half a joint a few weeks ago. I think he smokes huge quantities of
it, sitting in his room, on the internet or watching cricket, the
cannabis and methadone numbing him to the point of stupor – so
that he will not go out and be tempted by heroin. But he, along

with Andrés, is the most openly enthusiastic of them all and very keen to learn as much as possible, so any mood swings from him are very noticeable.

Chubby rotavated beds in tunnel and Andrés, Rocky and I sieved the pile of old compost that produced wonderful black stuff which Chubby rotavated in. For someone so thin and ethereal Andrés is an amazing worker. He is back to his best self again and this lifts the tenor of the entire place. The beds are now workable which is a huge step forward. We hitched up the rotavator onto the tractor and tried a strip across the ploughed field but it is still too wet – just round balls of clay.

Had meeting with David Chantler and Philip after the others had left to discuss Philip's future as his contract is up for renewal in two weeks' time. Lots of talk about budgets and how best to manage Philip's time. We went on talking round the subject until Philip announced that he would not be wishing to renew his contract in his present role. He was happy to consider a position managing a number of sites but not to continue the day-to-day stuff. He also did not want to continue part-time. He would not be renewing his contract on the terms offered. End of conversation.

This was a shock and does put us in a bit of a spot. David immediately rang Beth – someone who works with him on Ludlow Food Festival – to see if she would cover some lambing and Marsha is contacting Andy Trim to see if he can cover some veg work. Ideally David Reeve would formally do the morning and evening covering of animals, watering, trouble etc. – which would be fairly unarduous – but I think that it is unlikely at the moment.

Home after 7 p.m., in the dark. Checked my own chickens and greenhouses.

27/3/06

Long day. Went and picked up three gas canisters first thing for the heaters in the mess hut. I am sure it never crosses their mind where the heat comes from – only the absence of them if it is cold.

Then met crew at the Rock, recorded a few bits and then Andy Trim visited at 10.00. Showed him round and chatted with Philip in attendance. Clear *froideur* – but Philip has always been suspicious of Andy and his biodynamics. Andy is prepared to commit to two half days a week – ten till two – which will be a help but in no way covers Philip.

They finally arrived at 11 with just Andrés, Kate, Paul and Chubby. Chris Davies has a job, Andy B is ill – with hepatitis – and Chris Spires is still locked into heroin until he gets a script. Kate furious at news of Philip: I'm not happy Monty, not happy at all. And went and stood with a cup of tea in the middle of the yard, arms folded and feet close together. I haven't seen her for a fortnight and she looks ill – thin and very drawn. I tell her as much.

It's because I've been on gear she says. And that has made me ill. Why?

Cos I've lost my tolerance. Being off it.

Paul is truculent and bolshie in support of what he perceives as Philip's ill treatment. They all like him very much but they also all hate change. It threatens them. We have a coffee, talk about the deliveries – new propagating tunnel, seed boxes etc. – and set off to do rotas and put the tunnel up. I take Katie off to the tunnel for sowing once she has dragged herself away from Philip and the lambs. We sow spinach, leeks, chard, cabbage and beetroot in a raised bed as a seed bed (later, when the seeds come up, the ones she sowed were comically unstraight and chaotic. She was in a bad way that day). She shows me the ulcer/abscess on her leg. It is horrific – huge and black. Apparently there is another higher up.

Just from one dig she tells me. So my dad won't know I am using cos he checks my arms.

A 'dig' is an injection. Seeing her legs the description is horribly apt. It is a huge hole – a shell wound. She says she would like to have her leg amputated to get rid of the pain and scars.

How will I go on the beach with great purple scars? But then a bikini would look odd with one leg wouldn't it?

I have decided to give up the *Observer* and, after stiffening up my resolve, ring to tell them I am giving up my column after twelve years. I get an Answerphone. Such are the rewards for momentous decisions.

Lunch was leg of the Tamworth boar and was stunningly good. Given the problems we have had over the last week or so with Tricia and food this was an act of grace and felt like a gift. Chubby would not touch it and Paul went along with him, choosing a bacon bap. Only Kate and Andrés see a meal as an act of hospitality. The rest would be happiest eating a roll whilst standing or walking around, then having a fag and a cup of tea whilst sitting. Unlike Tom's furtive and anguished process of eating, they are perfectly benign about this – but sit at the table awkwardly and without relish. However it invariably works to some extent and by the end of the meal we are always talking around the table rather than at it. There is a huge difference.

Then back out into the rain to fiddle with the new polytunnel, fixing the base. I had to go to Leominster building supplies to get some coach screws, which I did with a camera crew. This process of doing the things that I often do – visiting the same shops, streets and portions of my non-telly world – is clearly crossing a line but in truth I do not mind. I never feel remotely self-conscious in front of a camera whereas I invariably feel nervous before an audience, even if only of half a dozen people.

The group wanted to stay and meet David Chantler to express their disgust at what they see as Philip being forced to resign but left easily enough. Between 4.30 and 7 p.m. David Chantler, David and Tricia and I had a filmed meeting in the shed. The Reeves had prepared a document for discussion covering food, work, the whole DTTO programme – but really to give Tricia a chance to express her feelings.

I found myself defending the group and praising their progress – whereas David and Tricia have become more hard line and less tolerant of them. Trish says that she is appalled that she had been misled about their drug taking.

The truth is that no one will give up heroin by coercion. Threaten them with punishment of some kind – withdrawal of privileges, prison, illness or death – and it never ever works. Tricia and David find this tricky. Any kind of reward is, in their eyes, only encouraging their turpitude. But all you can do is to create an environment in which they feel motivated and supported to choose to get off and stay off heroin. For all the reasons that they are on it in the first place, that will be difficult and slow. Sporadic reuse is very probable. Drugs – and perhaps more importantly the ritual of drug taking – are right at the centre of their lives. Remove it and there is a great yawning gap. It will be filled by something. What we are trying to do is provide something that could fill it in a rewarding way. There – the taboo word – reward.

Got home exhausted. Went to bed at eleven and woke at three churning things over. Got up at 4.30 to work. This bloody thing chews away at you.

27.03.06

Phillip's departure has left us all upset due to him being made to resign. Why should we have 2 new people? All this change is bollocks. We planted some of the raised beds today as well. All in all, a good day except Phillip's news. He will be missed.

Katie

31/3/06

I rang Philip from filming at 'Gardeners' World' to thank him for his involvement and to wish him well. He told me that on Wednesday only Paul came to the Rock. Andy B and Andrés were due but Andy B was in hospital with hepatitis – 'he's really bad. Apparently his urine is black' and Andrés had been picked up by the police on Tuesday for stealing three bars of chocolate.

This is terrible news.

It feels as though the whole thing is falling apart. Over the past few weeks:

1) Chris Spires addicted and dealing in heroin having come out of prison clean
2) Philip resigning
3) Rocky holiday
4) Tricia giving up food and both her and David withdrawing from the project to a degree
5) Kate ill, using heavily, hideous leg ulcers
6) Andy B seriously ill – probably out for weeks if not months
7) Andrés arrested – potentially in serious trouble and reverting to lost behaviour

The Andrés thing astonishes me. I really really cannot understand it – because he has so much to lose and almost nothing to gain. Or least that is what I assume. Perhaps he does not see it like that.

I mentioned this as I was leaving GW. 'You can't save everybody,' the director said dryly. No – but I badly want to save this lot.

April 2006

3/4/06

Busy day. Bought loaves of bread, pies, cheese, chutney and milk on way over. Later, Chris D opened the bags, saw the bread and asked what they were. Bread, I said. He looked surprised.

Andy Trim arrived in a well beaten-up trailer loaded with his home-made bed-maker which is two ploughs welded together so that they both turn the soil inwards. Then we had a prearranged visit from Sarah Humphries and her friend John Archer who have volunteered to check the place over morning and night every Thursday, Friday, Saturday and Sunday. I showed them round as everyone else turned up. The idea is that Andy Trim comes every Monday and Wednesday morning, I do every Tuesday and try and come as many Monday and Wednesday afternoons that I can, Beth Cohen comes on a Wednesday specifically to look after the sheep, Sarah Humphries does the feeding and watering over the weekend and I cover for them as and when needed. So it will take five people to replace Philip.

As I opened the tunnel for Sarah and John we disturbed a rabbit. It was large and panicky and repeatedly hurled itself at the sides, bouncing off back into the beds. Finally we chased it out the doors. If we get rabbits in the tunnel then we are in real trouble. They are not something that I have had too many problems with over the years but I have noticed an increase of them at home. I hope to God we don't have to fence against them as it is very expensive and laborious to do effectively.

Then David appeared saying that he had changed his mind and

wanted the new small propagating tunnel that we had started to put up moved to a new location. It was too visible in the yard. Even though we had put it specifically where David had told us to. This is difficult as it involves taking it down and thus undoing all the work that had only just been done. Much muttering from all involved. To his credit – and he has plenty of credit already accumulated to draw upon – David spent most of the day doing the hard work for this.

Andy B came – to my intense surprise – looking thin and wan but not too bad. He says that he does not have hepatitis but either a stomach ulcer or kidney trouble. Probably both. Despite his zaniness it is good to have him back. He is definitely one of the group. Immediately he asks if he can be a fireman today – collect wood for a fire. I say no, he must work with us as part of the team. What team? he asks.

He tells me that he was supposed to have a blood test but the nurse could not find a vein in his arms. Then he told them that he had never used in his legs so they should try there. No luck. No available vein. He said that he wanted to take the syringe and do it himself in the groin but they wouldn't let him. A surgeon was called but he could not do it. So he has to go back tomorrow.

Andrés and Paul dealt with the last two lambs, ringing balls and tails and then moved the four ewes and seven lambs out into the field. In the process they found the battery from the electric fence was missing which is odd and a bit worrying.

Rocky and I had a chat over the state of play. Rocky has returned from holiday tanned and looking well. He is slightly shocked at the chaos that has evolved in his absence but this is expressed with a raised eyebrow rather than overt alarm. As of next week he will come Monday, Tuesday and Wednesday and up the numbers, aiming at half a dozen each day.

Razor Paul is due to be allowed back (he was kicked out in September for suspicion of using in the loo here). Paul Mellor from Leominster has only fourteen days left on his order but wants to keep coming. I hope he does. I ask Tall Paul if he knows Little Paul – Razor? he says, Oh yeah I know him. We bumped into each other in prison. As though it were part of the social round. I suppose that it is for most of them. It is a mistake to think that they are not just as scared by things like prison as the rest of us. But they are battle-hardened. War-weary. They know what is coming, have worked out the best ways to deal with it and brace themselves. They are arch-survivors.

Lunch was good – a communal fry-up. Every scrap of bread was eaten with relish – the pies too. Andrés and I then went into Leominster to get a battery – without film crew in tow. I asked him what had happened last week when he got arrested. He said that he had been drunk, walked into a shop and saw an off-duty policeman (they must know all the police in Worcester), picked up three chocolate bars, waved them at him and walked out of the shop. The guy – not unreasonably – ran after him and arrested him for the theft. He was taken to the cells and left there overnight. The next day he went before the magistrates and was fined £40. End of story.

It begs a million questions. Why ask for trouble so blatantly? Why risk everything for so little? How much is he drinking? A lot. From nine in the morning. When he starts he can't stop. He hasn't taken heroin for two months but the drink is getting hold. Why tantalise the copper? Because the worm will always turn. Waving three bars of chocolate before walking off with them is two fingers at oppression and two cheers for that. Why arrest him and keep him overnight in the cells? Because that tends to happen if you break the law at night and are clearly drunk. Why charge him and fine him £40? Because he has a record that stretches beyond counting and the law is vengeful. His real crime – and life-affirming act – was to mock them.

With a battery attached the electric fence felt a better bet.

When I got back everyone was standing round the tractor and bed-maker in the field with that hands-in-pockets, teeth-sucking stance that invariably goes with a breakdown. Andy's bed-maker had broken.

But it turns out that Andy B is a good welder so he will mend it next week. I'll bring in my mask he said. And I'll get a beaver for the pond. His strangeness is benign and almost reassuring.

I helped Chubby and Chris and Andrés muck out the lambing shed – we moved five trailer loads of manure and perhaps three more to go. In the process Chris ripped a gate off its hinges but rehung it competently enough – although the other way round. It is David's gate, not ours, but David seemingly unbothered by this. Chris was certainly untroubled.

They left and I watered the tunnel and waited for visitors that never came. I had got the wrong day. But a good day really for its comforting mundaneness and rhythm.

Paul Mellor said that he used the other day the first time for ages. A friend told me he had terminal cancer. So I did the only thing I know how to do and went and got some gear and used. Then when I told him he said You stupid cunt. That made me realise that I don't need to use. I feel strong now.

I am not sure that I believe him, but I hope I am maligning him. There is something very vulnerable and decent about him.

I am aware that this diary will be read by them. It curtails me yet being dishonest feels like a waste of time, although honesty never won any friends.

8/4/06

I open Leominster allotments. The film crew are there plus local BBC crew plus the *Observer* who have sent a reporter all the way from London. He is late (no one ever knows how far Herefordshire is from London) and it never makes the paper. I love everything about allotments and this site, made from a field at the edge of town, is great. Families raking in the bright sun and icy wind. I love the way that country towns still are bounded by fields. Tractors go down the High Street. This counters the anonymity of suburbia – yet suburbia, like it or not, is where most people live. If the project is to spread and have meaning it must do so to those in the suburbs too. Perhaps we should take an allotment or two.

The Mayor of Leominster and Mayor of Hereford are there, supportive and friendly about the project. I speak proudly of what we are achieving and say it is going well. I am lying. I don't think that it is going well. I think it is surviving – just. I am aware that I am lazy and not doing what must be done – setting up the foundation to keep things going. I long for someone to take this out of my hands yet feel possessive.

Go home and write all day feeling fraudulent and unequal to the task. I suspect that there is a streak of vanity gnawing at the heart of this and I will pay for that.

10/4/06

I went over to the Rock intending to stay just for an hour, have a cup of tea, chat over what was to be done and leave. I bought five loaves of bread, four pies, flapjacks, cheese and butter on the way. Met Andy there – beautiful day, clear blue sky. The first since last October. The place looked terrific and last Wednesday they had made raised beds with the rotavator and planted out the beans and garlic that we grew in pots. Both filled a whole bed. It was a fabulous sight. Fab site. Everything seemed possible. In the polytunnel all seeds had germinated and mizuna and rocket ready for pricking out. The seeds that Katie had sowed on her own were crazy – pools and fingers of seed across the bed.

Andy Trim and I planned the day whilst waiting for them – planting potatoes, putting up the propagating tunnel, sowing peas and beans. Using the soil and weather. Taking the moment with both hungry hands.

We waited for them to turn up. And waited and waited. Finally, at 11.15 I said I had to go and as I was leaving Rocky arrived – alone. Kate was supposed to be with him but 'she has big issues'. I didn't really know what this meant but nodded. Her methadone has been lowered which is a total disaster. Rocky was shocked that the others were not there. At 11.30 we rang and Andrés said he was alone driving down the motorway. In fact they were in a shop buying milk in Bromyard – ten miles away.

The sun shone. The dry soil crisped slightly. Above all I was aware how pecious the day was and how little was going to get done before the forecast rain. Finally they did arrive – nonchalant and unapologetic. I set them up and left, fuming. Spent the rest of the day writing but did not start until 12.30.

11/4/06

I picked up eight sacks of chicken feed on my way in.

Just Tony, Jack, Andrés and Paul arrived today. Kate has got an interview, Chubby not well, Chris D getting an emergency loan, Andy B at the dentist (he's got roots all tangled up), Barrie had gone to have a haircut when they arrived to pick him up. (Barrie? – apparently one of the Wheelchair Gang. That is its real name. His brother had to have a leg amputated after over injecting into it so was in a wheelchair but still wanted to go thieving with them. Their main claim to fame was robbing an entire warehouse of its contents over many months by entering from the back and leaving the front untouched. No one noticed until at last they worked their way forward and removed the remaining front layer of stuff to reveal an empty warehouse). Chris Spires unable to cope until he has a script and Razor Paul not yet on.

It rained from morning until twenty minutes before they left early at 3.45 (Paul had to go and sign on). Despite (because of?)

the low turnout it was a good day. I put Tony and Jack onto the new polytunnel which they struggled with in the rain all day, and I spent the day with Andrés and Paul. We checked all the fences. (I take a call from the *Guardian* about the hosepipe ban, as I did so 'Just a couple of questions: would you say that Britain is a very *gardening* country?') Then we transplanted a bed full of mizuna and another of rocket whilst Paul thinned all the direct sown seedlings. He did it beautifully. He said that this was what he really wanted to join the project for – growing and learning things.

At lunch – very cosy with the heater on in the barn and the rain and wind battering on the tin roof – our own sausage sandwiches and mugs of tea – we talked about the future and getting away from drugs. A week ago a man came up to Andrés in Worcester, in the middle of the day, and punched him in the face. What did you think when that happened? I asked.

That it was a bloody good one, he replied. He caught me proper.

It turned out that the man thought Andrés was responsible for maligning him to mutual acquaintances. When he found out that was completely untrue he sought him out and shook his hand. What did he think of *that*? I asked. That I'm never going back to that flat again, he said. The punch was hard enough to make him go to casualty 'and wait for ages and ages' to have an X-ray that revealed a hairline fracture. Life went on.

This is the world that both are keen to get away from. It is not just dealers and crime but violence, mistrust and fear. Dog eat dog. I asked Andrés about the guy that he had spent the night with sleeping rough on the street in freezing weather to protect him. He is now sleeping under the stairs outside the hostel apparently.

I went and put some Scotch pancakes under his sleeping bag last night. So he would have something to eat when he woke up like.

This kind of tenderness is astonishing. I know of no one from the straight world who modestly and regularly does acts of this kind. Yet Andrés is officially a hopeless criminal and addict. He was given his order – effectively prison – of eighteen months for stealing a ten-pound object. The other day a man was given eight months for killing a pedestrian on a level crossing, uninsured and driving away. The only justice that they respect and employ is a natural one. But they are extraordinarily benign and tolerant of the police and courts. There is a sense that they are only doing their jobs.

Andrés has been clean for two months now. The longest he can remember. Certainly the longest outside prison. He said that when he came to the project he had no script so was still using. It was terrible. He coped by putting his gear safely in his room so it was there for him when he got back. Knowing it was there saw him through the day. If he had not had any waiting he could not have done it. Paul said You're like me. You'll be terrible, really terrible but when a dealer puts a wrap in your hand you immediately feel better.

Paul said that he liked prison. It was clean, there was no violence in category C, there was no heroin, the food was good, he had lessons and counselling and he was drug free. His parents liked it too as their own lives got back to normal. Life was much harder on the outside. He longed to play sport again and would love to join a cricket team. In my book, anyone who likes cricket has their heart in the right place. He has a treadmill in his bedroom to keep fit. What he really liked about the project – other than learning stuff – was seeing us all, talking to someone, sharing the same things and having friends. It gave him his social life. and meant that he could get out without using.

Paul mainly injected in the groin so his parents wouldn't know and he could wear shorts. You can always tell a smackhead in summer because he's the one wrapped up in layers of clothes.

After lunch we pricked out eight trays (each of thirty-five

plugs) of cocarde and little leprechaun lettuce. Then it was time for them to go.

It was a good day with people I like very much.

12/4/06

Went in for a few hours, stopping off to buy two bags of pig nuts and two chicken pies, to meet Beth who is starting to do a Wednesday each week, primarily to run the sheep. We agreed that we should sell all but half a dozen ewes, each with twins. The situation at the moment is that there is no grass for them so they will need feeding with nuts and hay for at least another month if not more. Beth noted that the lambs were an extraordinary mixed bunch – implying that the ram(s) must have been equally idiosyncratic. In order to sell them we need tags, a holding number and the records of their births. I, of course, have no idea where or what these are and Philip certainly left no instructions nor ever discussed them.

Andy Trim and I talked through the sowing programme. At the moment though it feels like everyone is waiting for me to tell them what to do. I don't mind this but it would be nice to unload that.

Again only Andrés and Paul turned up – all others absent with honourable excuses but it is a trifle worrying. We need to have a core of half a dozen that we can rely on and – importantly – that build up some ability and knowledge. Just being there is increasingly not enough.

25/4/06

Combination of Easter and five days in Mallorca mean that I have not been there with them for a fortnight. (Although I was there three times over Easter feeding the animals and doing the tunnel etc.)

Andy B, Kate, Andrés, Paul and Chris D came. It was genuinely good to see them. It was also a genuinely sunny spring day – the first nice weather since September. Everything seemed possible. The polytunnel was fully planted up with salad crops and we can start harvesting next week and Kate had sown about twenty seed trays supervised by Andy Trim.

Andrés and Paul are a team – focused, tall, fast moving and both fearful. This fear is, I think, mostly about loss, but they both look a little hunted. Nevertheless they now almost run the place and are completely engaged, especially with the animals and daily tasks of keeping things moving forward. At various stages of the day they fed all the animals, moved the pig (it was good to see her too. She is now as tame as a great fat dog) into the lambing barn, securing it first and putting down a carpet of straw, tidied up her old quarters and moved it all to the compost area, watered in long rows of plants, which involved one of them pointing the hose and the other holding two sections together in lieu of a coupling. This inevitably meant the holder getting soaked.

Chris and Jack spent the morning trying to fix the cooker. In the end it defeated them because they couldn't get the right parts for the connection. But it involved trips to Leominster where I bumped into them a few times. Chris has an absolute focus on the job in hand – until it goes and then its absence is absolute. It is an off and on switch. He is puffy with drink and finding it hard to get a job but of all of them he is the one that will get on and do something best – especially if it involves making something – but around half past three he is itchy to be off. In the afternoon he started making staging for the new polytunnel (put up in my absence) and was doing really well but when I went to see it in the evening the tools and piece of wood he had been sawing were dropped and the whole thing left like the *Marie Celeste*. The attention had been switched off.

It was the first time that Andy B has visited for a while. The big news is that he finally had a blood test (two nurses and a surgeon failed to find a vein. In the end he took it himself in his groin) and yesterday they called him in to tell him that he does not have hepatitis. But he has kidney and liver failure and is to be treated for that. He also has to have seven teeth taken out next week under general anaesthetic. He is to see a psychologist today who is to give him 'tablets for me head'. He told me that there are three different people inside him. He tries to ignore one of them that tells him to do stupid things like take smack. One, I guess, is the Andy I see and the third was 'Private. I'm not going to talk about it. It's between me'. He said that he had been using for fourteen years – since he was just thirteen. He said before that it was eleven 'but that's because it WAS eleven so I just stuck with that. But of course it's not eleven no more'. He is twenty-seven.

He worked well all day, very carefully weeding the seed beds with minute attention to detail. He is very good at this, thinning seedlings and replanting them as he goes. I like him very much although it is hard to communicate with him, not least because of his deafness.

Kate – who I had also not seen for a while – is in a bad way. She looks stiff and taut as though her body is stretched too tightly around her. She owes her dealer 330 quid and doesn't know where to get the money. Apparently she has already had a 'slap'.

I took Kate with me to do some shopping (typically I had to organise getting wood for building staging for the propagating tunnel, sheep feed, a fitting to connect the gas cooker and chicken pies for lunch). On the journey she was at her best, bright, rude, funny and indomitable. I asked why she was using sufficiently seriously to run up this kind of debt – although for all I know it is just one she happens to talk about. She said it was because she was frightened. What of? Everything. I couldn't work out whether this was a self-pitying stock reply or genuine. Probably both. Why was she using crack again? I'm not really. Just for a treat now and then. It is a depressingly predictable story. She uses crack, inevitably wants more, has no money so the dealer gives her some and says she can pay for it when she has money. This goes on all day. The next day he comes looking for his money and starts charging interest and using threats from that point.

When we got back she changed into a truculent, displaced teenager, bolshie and deeply unhappy. Her ulcers are infected, her stomach bloated and not holding food and she is not really up to any work. At lunch she demanded a big bit of quiche, took a mouthful and said it was skank. There was the familiar 'why can't we have normal, supermarket food?' Everyone else teases her about this – which in itself is a huge indication of how things have moved forward – but she is clearly truly unhappy and her longing for 'normal' anything is profound and hopeless. Nevertheless she showed me all the seeds that she had sown the day before, with Andy Trim, with great pride.

I find all this deeply upsetting, like watching someone drown just yards from the shore.

Rocky took her to the doctor in the afternoon and then brought her back to the steering group meeting at seven. She appeared to be out of her head, blanked off, starting conversations with no relevance to anything else being said, getting up and walking around, dropping things, a caricature of the dangerous junkie. In fact she had apparently taken antibiotics and had a drink with the others at the pub and the mix, along with methadone, was making her behave like this. She verbally attacked David Chantler, the chief probation officer, for Philip's absence, seeing it as a conspiracy worked upon him. 'We are drug addicts and we don't like change.' Again it was too trite and easy and not very convincing although true.

Rocky is clearly worried about her and how long she can sustain her own equilibrium and also the effect on the others. It is interesting to see how upsetting this kind of element is to the group. They want steadiness and security and one person can disrupt all that – yet the one disruptive person probably needs the safety and security more than the others.

In fact none of the locals turned up for the steering group. David Reeve went through the motions of chairing it in rather a formal way but it was really a display for David Chantler. We agreed to go along with whatever we could produce to the Canon Pyon fête on 20 May and to have a barbecue/open evening on 31 May.

Just as the meeting was about to begin Paul came rushing over, Where's our pig? Someone's nicked the pig! We ran over and the barn was empty. There was no sign of a forced exit. We finally found her, happy as a pig in a puddle, in the muddy ditch that we cleared a few months ago. She did not run far but let us go over and scratch her behind the ears. There was a bit of a freedom scamper but then she followed a bucket of nuts willingly enough back into the barn. Paul and Andrés then found and blocked the bolt hole. David Reeve was most perplexed by this irregular behaviour. In fact it was a lovely few moments, all of us running towards the same end. Only Kate seemed unaware what was going on.

We showed David Chantler around and Kate was rifling through the seed packets looking for things to take home. She asked if she could pick the sweet peas. Not yet I said.

But they're dying Mont, she said, they ain't got no flowers.

No not yet Kate. The flowers will come later. It's not time yet.

Can I pick them anyway to take to my dad?

Not yet Kate, not yet. The sweet peas, you – us – are not ready yet.

Re-reading the daybook I see that Katie is the only one who regularly signs her full name: Katie Hirschfield. Often she puts K. Hirschfield. There is a real sense of identity in that.

So I google 'Kate Hirschfield'. It is all there. In March 2001, police followed her from a park in Worcester to the home she shared with her boyfriend. He was apparently unable to leave his bed, and asked Katie to hand over a wrap of heroin worth £25 to a man who came to the door. The police then arrested this man and charged Katie with supplying heroin. They also found another heroin wrap under a carpet in the hall, together with £175. The court decided to be lenient and gave her a deferred sentence as a 'messenger', which was then substituted by a drug treatment and testing order in an effort to address her battle with heroin addition. But in a pattern I had become familiar with, Katie had found the drug therapy difficult and her attendance was poor. She continued to use, and supported this with shoplifting. Eventually, despite pleas from her defence councel to continue with therapy that he believed was helping, the judge had no choice but to impose a custodial sentence and she was sent to prison for 16 months. She was 22.

Then I check the Worcester war memorials for Hirschfield and find this from World War I.

HIRSCHFIELD. E.
HIRSCHFIELD. F.
HIRSCHFIELD. F.
HIRSCHFIELD. T.

Katie's relatives? How many different unrelated Hirschfields would there have been in Worcester over the past 100 years? And why the Germanic name in the middle of provincial England? The point being not that she is shaming the memory of those that died for their country (probably in mud, blood and utter pointless despair) but that she is rooted in the past of this place. Belonging matters. All the connections matter. The names on a war memorial are saying exactly the same thing as the plants that grow from a particular soil. We all matter. We all belong somewhere.

I remember, many years ago, chatting to a man whilst waiting for the ferry to Mull and asking where he came from and he replied in the lovely singsong of the Highlands and islands, 'My people belong to Gigha' which at the time – and now – I thought one of the most beautiful and poetic ways of describing one's roots. I now know that this is how almost any Scots will say where their home is. For many of us this is impossible. We do not necessarily feel that our people 'belong' anywhere or that we belong with them. For all the pity of that I also believe that you can arrive at where you belong and that this can be a subtle and diverse thing. But it matters terribly to find out where that is.

May 2006

2/5/06

Spring has been cold and hesitant but May – lovely lovely May – is at last here and the entire countryside is exhaling, breathing green. The blossomest blossom ever. Like arriving at shore after a winter at sea.

Again rushing around shopping – bags for salad, fair trade tea and coffee, bread, three-quarter-inch hose fitting, rotavator (collected from friend I had lent it to), printing job rotas. I went assuming that the rabbit netting would be there but it had not been delivered. So that had to be chased up. I loathe this administrative organisation and am hopeless at it. Long for someone else to do it.

I asked Kate about her behaviour the other night at the meeting and she had no memory of it at all. I can remember being there but nothing I done. She had, she said, taken some Seconal (? wrong name). Why? Was it an antibiotic? No it's an anti-psychotic. Why do you take that?

I always take it when I get home.

Why?

It calms me down like. Relaxes me.

She potted up tomatoes with a furious speed.

Apparently she used yesterday but would not talk to me about it. But she was well and very involved with the seeds – but not taking part in the more physical stuff, going off with Rocky in the morning to do some shopping. The truth is that she is not physically up to any sustained work. She is an invalid.

There was a moment after lunch when Barrie was driving the tractor with great skill, gathering topsoil and tipping it into the raised beds to top them up, Chris D and Paul were both rotavating the same beds, Andrés was taking out barrowloads of weed and Rocky was helping and all were wholly focused on their work, all working hard and well in an integrated fashion on the same project. It was perfect.

Barrie has been a couple of times before but today was the first whole day that I had spent with him. He has a glazed, absent look but could pass for sixteen, seventeen. Almost innocent. He is, apparently, far from it. He had the body language and attitude that they all had when they came – wouldn't sit with us, standing apart from any group activity, only really engaged when driving the tractor, not joining in any discussions. But he is very likeable and worked hard and well – despite disappearing without comment at one point when we were weeding the beds. I went to find him after about fifteen minutes and he was reading a paper. What's up Barrie? Oh I was just having a rest.

At lunch he sat separately smoking a fag and watching us eat.

Come on Barrie, come and sit with us.

Nah.

Why not? What's the problem?

Nothing. I'm just chillin.

Chill with us.

Nah. I don't like sitting at a table when other people are eating. I sit when I get my food (the food was on the table although Rocky was frying him an egg). Sure enough he ate his egg sitting at the table but as far away from anyone else as possible then immediately got up and went back to his seat in the corner.

Food has been a problem for every one of them in some form or other. It is, I guess, all about control. When the world is chaotic then imposing controls – however destructive or banal – on food seems to happen. An easy carelessness and curiosity about food comes with security and confidence that the un-known is not hostile. But the disparity between what they are prepared to ingest chemically compared to their suspicion and conservatism about food – not to say downright ignorant stupidity – is always astonishing.

Nevertheless, today we had our first vegetable harvest. We picked mizuna and rocket from the tunnel and they each took a bag home. There was not a lot of enthusiasm for this – certainly no sense of celebration – but that is all of a piece. There is no joy in their lives.

Chris Davies has a job, making rope. This is a triumph for him and we get some reflected glory. Certainly of all of them he is the one that fulfils the least of one's expectations and preconceptions of a heroin addict. It seems as though he slipped into addiction almost by accident. But there were times when Tom was around when he seemed a really difficult case – hostile to the project and holding too much in reserve to reach. We shall really miss him and his skills; he is our handyman and has done more than anyone to physically set the place up. But every expression of praise and hope is tempered by anxiety – I am beginning to share the addict's fear of failure that increases the further you get away from full-on involvement.

We had a visit from Fordhall farm in the afternoon. They had wanted us to buy all/some shares in their farm so that the project could be extended up there. We rejected this because it is too far from us to be the base we want and also we would want somewhere entirely under our control. But they could start a project site up there themselves. They are young, bright and very resourceful. In fact I forgot to talk to them about this. It is too distracting having visitors during the working day. Like having a work meeting whilst looking after a group of toddlers. But they do have a Gloucester Old Spot boar which we could mate with our Tamworth.

I got home at five thirty absolutely shattered. Could hardly walk. This group suck the shreds of energy from me.

187

03.05.06

Today is my last day on the farm and I am gonna miss the place but I have to move on and up. So, saying goodbye and leaving is only the beginning so I hope all goes well and hope to see you all soon.

Thanks to Monty, Andy, Beth, David and Trish and cheers to all the team and a special thanks to Mr Robert Hudson who without I would not have gotten this far. Cheers mate!

See ya – Chrisx

Good luck in the future Chris. Today has been good. Saw a 2 foot Grass Snake near the pond.

Andrés Pope

Getting accurate figures to research this has been difficult. What follows are government figures.

It is reckoned that there are about 250,000 regular heroin users, each spending about £10,000 a year to supply their habit. That is about two and a half billion a year.

The police say that the resale value of stolen goods is one third or less. So it amounts to crime of about 10 billion a year of retail value. The cost of insurance and the bureaucracy involved must add to that.

The cost of police, legal aid, courts, social services, probation and prison for youth crime (i.e. under twenty-one) is estimated to be between £5 billion and £10 billion (how can it vary by 100 per cent?) Given that all my lot are over twenty-one let us go for the upper estimate.

Let's call it a modest £20 billion

According to a report on Youth Crime to the House of Commons in 2004 it costs:

£164,750 per child aged 15–17 to place them in a Secure Training Centre.

£50,800 per adult aged 18–20 in a Young Offenders institution.

For adults it is generally reckoned to cost about £35,000 per year to keep them in prison.

This scheme is costing less than £100 a day per person. Call it £500 per week. That is about £25k per year per person. They have drug testing and court reviews on top of that. Allow for the wasteful inefficiency of bureaucracy and call it another £10k a year. During that period they commit next to no crimes and their drug use falls hugely.

Even the most cynical observer cannot deny that it is a very cheap way of keeping them out of trouble and saves the taxpayer huge sums of money.

8/5/06

To Manchester to talk to a symposium about food in the city. The council are taking extraordinarily far-reaching and far-sighted steps to improve the sustainability and quality of the food in Manchester, covering markets, delivery, schools, old people's homes, institutions, hospitals etc. I tell them about the project and our attempts to connect food to place and community – and our struggles with getting the group to accept any kind of food outside their prior experience or to see it as a bonding social experience. Good response. I always do get a good response when I go out and talk about it. I must get out more – it is easy to become dejected or just plain exhausted when you stay too close to it. And my role in the end must be to enable the big picture.

I am shown a city farm and am envious of the purpose built

buildings they have. But we could do that. If we got our own space we could create somewhere that worked right for us and that people could visit. I wish the group had been with me to see it.

The next day I only popped in briefly to see them. They were due to tag sheep in the afternoon before they go off for sale because we have no grass and have run out of hay. If we sell half of them we can keep on feeding them the hugely expensive feed until the grass starts to grow.

I tell them about Manchester and the fascinating stuff that I heard about behaviour and diet which directly relates to them. They did show a tiny bit of polite interest but I guess that if you are prepared to load your system with 30 bags of heroin a day the behaviour-related effect of your diet is not the top of your priorities.

Aparently Paul and Andy Trim had a ding dong yesterday but I could not gather what it was about. No one seems that bothered about it.

09.05.06

Sorry I haven't been to the farm. I aint been very well but getting better. You all will be seeing more of me from now on. Thanks for all your support while I was away but I aint missed much apart from the plants have grown more and Beth started (nice girl!?)

Andy B

Today has been a good day all round. Tagged the sheep and lambs and a bit of planting. Tomorrow some ewes and lambs go off to be sold.

Andrés 2006

Today has been a brilliant day but saying that, everyday is a good day on the farm. Today we have been tagging the sheep ready for market tomorrow. I would also like to apologise to Andy and to everyone who witnessed my childlike outburst which was wrong of me to do.

SO SORRY!

Paul

Good days seem to be coming now all the time you all seem to be improving health wise and eating well. We are getting busier and eating the first of our crops. We have introduced ourselves to Fiona at Grove Farm shop and hopefully we will be doing some swaps with our produce. Paul, thank you for your apology. It is accepted – no worries mate – you and everyone else make sure you keep enjoying the farm and your lives. Cheers everyone. Keep going.

Rocky

12/5/06

The briefest of notes written at 7 a.m. in a bus on the road between Granada and Cordoba, a BBC crew sleeping around me.

The team came to the Malvern Spring Show a couple of days ago, as much for a day out as any serious learning process. They seemed to like it. I liked showing them a bit of my world outside the farm and also being able to give them privileged access to things – especially as people were looking at them sideways. In fact I thought that they blended in fine but I have obviously gone native because I overheard one of the runners talking to another about them. Where are they? the one asked. Down by the show gardens, the second answered. How will I recognise them? Oh you'll recognise them all right.

This, of course, is the problem. They instantly spot the white trousers, trainers and brown teeth but that obscures almost everything else about them.

I introduced Andrés to an especially nice Well Known Person who happened to be visiting although he has nothing to do with gardening on television. They talked politely for five minutes. The WKP then left, having been charming, unpatronising and thoroughly decent. When he was out of earshot Andrés said, He was a user.

How do you know? I said.

You can always tell Andrés said. It's something about the way they look. It was probably long ago but you can still tell.

The WKP was busy signing autographs, his past unrecognised by anyone save Popey.

15/5/06

I went over to see them, having got back from three days filming in Spain the night before. Andy Trim was there, Rocky, Kate, Andrés, Paul. Two policemen from Hereford, working in the same line as Rocky, were visiting and chatting to Paul about the possibility of him working part-time checking the animals. Kate was furious.

Why should he get a fucking job when I've been here since day one?

I point out that she lives thirty miles away and has no transport. She is on an order and he has finished his. She is still using energetically, doesn't really like the animals and is almost crippled with ulcers and a bad stomach. She hates getting her hands dirty. None of this cuts much ice. Anyone else's gain in the group is her loss.

Fucking bastard cunt she says. It's not fucking fair.

Her sense of grievance is acrid in the room.

Rocky is cooking a joint of beef, roast potato and three veg. These from the farm shop in return for the lettuces we gave them. It is a good deal. A general sense of being a gainer. We are up.

The police, male and female, are friendly, fit and keen to start something similar near Hereford. I think I was not enthusiastic enough. The truth is that I am generally a bit suspicious of all outsiders. On the whole they do not help a lot. But I think these two were potentially great.

Andrés tells me that Andy Trim thinks the pig is pregnant. Look at her teats he says. Andy T thinks she might be due any day. Gestation is 3 months and 3 weeks and 3 days. Could be due in three days or 3 weeks. It seems that she has been quietly growing piglets all spring.

I leave with a list in my notebook:

- Watering can
- Small rotavator
- RABBIT NETTING
- Plant out leeks/chard
- Muck on ground and rotovate
- Strimmer
- Timber for raised bed for piglets 40ft 9 × 1 or shuttering ply, 4 sheets.

I forget the watering can and the rotavator, discover that there is no rabbit netting because I was supposed to order it and didn't, the leeks, chard and muck are jobs for Tuesday, I bring in two mowers and strimmer but no petrol for any of them and the ply is ordered and comes next day. They deliver and charge me for 5 sheets. I do inspiration, not management. Sack me.

16/5/06

I spent all day at the Rock, working outside with Andrés, Paul, Andy B and Barrie (Hi Barrie, all right? I hold out a manly hand. He takes it limply and averts his eyes, Yeah. I have not seen him for about three weeks. What you been doing? Nothing. Nothing at all? Nothing). We move manure to the ploughed area and then rotavate it in. Then plant out the seedling leeks in two long rows. I am very aware as we do this, handling the grass-like seedlings with filigree roots, parting the heavy soil with my hands and slotting each leek seedling into place, that this is what I do best and that we are all sharing something we want to do and care about. It is immensely, almost dangerously, satisfying.

Tony (along with Jack, one of the two probation service drivers and helpers on the scheme) helped draw the drills with a mattock. What's that you're planting? he said. Leeks. Yuck! I hate leeks. All slimy. He is nearly sixty-seven and as fit as a butcher's dog. He has never cooked anything in his life.

Spoke a lot to Andy B who was in particularly surreal mood all day. He is very like an acid casualty, his mind making connections where there are none and failing to join things that seem inevitably yoked.

I like a strong woman to beat me he said. It hurts at the time but it's nice too. I like to see the grass cut properly and I can't have a job because I need a hearing aid.

He certainly does but refuses to get one – I might hear things I don't like.

He likes neatness and order.

My nan says to me, How can you be so tidy in your things like and so scruffy in yourself? I don't know. It's strange. But I can't bear things in the wrong place. They've got to be where I want them.

Tell me something, he said. Why has the pig got fourteen tits? She might only have one piglet. I say that women often have only one baby but usually have two breasts.

Two's nicer than one he says as though that explains the mystery of all those piggy teats.

You think I'm thick, but I'm not. I assure him I don't and I mean it. Odd, but not thick. He wanted to weed.

I wants to work in my own box, not bothering anyone else.

I had him cutting grass most of the day. It was his own box of sorts. It all looked fresh and cared for. He said that he hadn't used for seventeen days. Just an amp of methadone that he injected last week. He is addicted to injecting himself. That has carried me through like. The others – pharmaceutical experts that they all are – pointed out that this would have left his system after three days at the most, so it can't have done the trick. This immediately deflated him.

I've done well. Leave me alone. I'm doing well.

Paul says he is really happy we are going to have piglets.

At lunch Andrés has made a salad with spinach leaves draped over the side of the casserole dish. It is beautiful. Tricia has made a really excellent pizza. Andy B won't eat any of this but has a lettuce sandwich. For the first time ever there is a moment of satisfied silence as everyone is busy eating. It is an absolute measure of success.

17/5/06

Chubby's name is Darren. For some reason this feels a little shocking, as though he was Tarquin or Justin. Both perfectly good names – as is Darren – but not remotely tagged to Chubby. In the past five months I have not heard him called anything but Chubby, Chubbs or Chub. Jack told me that he had been arrested on Friday night for stealing a car. He also had some amphetamines in his pocket. After a night in the cells it transpired that he was not driving and one of the three arrested had 'borrowed' it from a friend. They had no proof of this but the friend might provide the necessary alibi. The speed is not a good move for Chubby but he should be free to come back to the project. Chubby is a decent person and a good bloke to have around but he is a stupid thing waiting to happen. A deep reluctance to grow up. He is the one who will always squirt you with water if he has a hosepipe or flick compost down someone's neck if we are potting up. If you shout at him – and I do – he will say Only having a bit of fun Mont. Just a bit of fun. But you always feel with him that it is fun poised to go wrong.

I popped over this morning with Marsha, meaning to stay for perhaps half an hour. Breeze in and breeze out. On our way we stopped to pick up rabbit netting, which we had been told was in stock and waiting collection. Nothing there. Nah. We don't keep that kind of thing in stock see. But you said . . . Not me, love. Anyway, I ordered it and the rabbits have a few more days buffet of our veg.

When we got to the Rock Andrés, Paul, Beth and Dean were having a cup of coffee, plus a probation officer. Slacking? I said, only slightly joking. No, Andrés and Paul almost chorused in a kind of Famous Five way, we are not allowed to touch the soil. Bog off. Honest! It's true, Andy Trim says.

It turns out that biodynamically the soil should not be turned or serviced in any kind of way today. So coffees all round. Beth was keen to worm the sheep but this, done prophylactically would break the organic code. So I said no. The truth is I couldn't care less if the filthy sheep had worms or not but I do care about casual, ad hoc breaching of the organic code. It shows that she sees it as a system to be obeyed only up to the point of convenience, rather than a philosophy. We agreed to do it when and if they got worms.

Beth had organised for friends of hers with shearing equipment to come in the afternoon to shear and show how to shear. The electric fence had been moved and the sheep rounded up into the pig pen for easy capture. I forgot to ask what will happen to the fleeces. Damn. That kind of thing is important.

Then Paul told me that the probation officer was changing the rota and taking most of the existing team off. This was such startling and potentially terrible news I hardly reacted at all. It took about five minutes to sink in. So I went off with the probation officer and tried to be chatty about it but quickly found myself getting angry.

I will do anything legal, I said, to stop you or anyone else doing this. To break up the team now would be an act of vandalism.

But we have fifty people waiting to come to The Farm she said. We only have limited transport. I had visions of a queue of offenders traipsing out here to have their 'farm' script.

And, she said, they are becoming too dependent. There are other things for them to learn. They need to be weaned off The Farm. (It annoys me to hear it referred to as The Farm. This is irrational and just possibly a bit snotty. But the irritation is there.)

I said that she obviously had no idea what we were doing and that nothing would be more harmful or counterproductive. I asked if she had spoken to David Chantler. No. She had not. She had never spoken to David about The Farm. Did she know what we were doing here?

Not really.

Then why, I resisted saying, are you coming in here and trying to fuck everything up?

I realised that she was someone trying to do her job as well as she could with the resources available to her. She obviously wished the project no harm. But it is typical of the broken-down, confused, misguided way that these things are run. It outrages me.

I promised Andrés that he could come three days a week for as long as he wanted and that no one would be cut back against their will. I have absolutely no idea if I can keep that promise but I will try.

No Kate. She did not come yesterday either. She apparently rang to say that her leg was bleeding and she needed to see the nurse (which nurse?). I thought that when Rocky was away she might fall back. It is a pity. I shan't see her now until the beginning of June. Of all of them she is the one who could most easily go under.

Andy Trim, as hale and raffish as a grower might be, was there. He is exactly the right counterblast to the rather solemn, well-meaning presence of probation officers or workers. In the morning he and the boys had made an enclosure within the barn for the sow to farrow in. She is pregnant, spotted by Andy on Monday. This is, despite the incest with her brother before he went to the butcher (we are steadily eating our way through him), a good thing, meaning we have potentially our own little herd of Tamworths. But first-time sows are notoriously bad mothers and should really be watched all the time. But for most of the day and all the night there is no one to do the watching. So we hope against hope that she farrows whilst we are there.

Away now for a fornight with a tangle of filming at GW, Chelsea and Morocco for a week. It seems a ridiculous time to be away. But it has always been like this. Around this time of year I never want to be anywhere but the British countryside and preferably as near to home as possible.

20/5/06

I got a phone call yesterday from Sarah Humphries – our weekend feed and watering cover – to see if I could cover her on Saturday night with the animals. As it happens I cannot – an eightieth birthday party to go to – but then she said And the piglets are lovely! They will be I said. No, she said, they are here!

So I rang Andy Trim to tell him that the pig had farrowed, with six piglets. I know he said. They came yesterday afternoon. Paul went over and Popey and the film crew and I went over in the evening to check them.

Whilst I am delighted, it feels like a party to which I was not invited. No one thought to tell me. I shall go over today and see them. Piglets eh? That feels like a triumph. The difference between buying lettuce from a farmers' market and growing them oneself. Our own piglets.

22.05.06

The weather has been awful. Have terrible toothache. The piglets are beautiful. The farm looks great.

AP 2006

24.05.06

Don't feel too good today. Hope to feel on track next week.

AP 2006

Been away a week, lots of changes! All good. Thank you everyone. Keep it up. Best wishes.

Rocky

The farm is really starting to look good with all of the plants/ vegetables coming through. I'm still enjoying myself and am learning something new everyday.

Paul

30/5/06

Spent last week in Marrakech, the weekend ill and first visit today for what feels like ages. In fact spent the first hour of the day replying to an email from the probation officer, which was sent to David Chantler, the chief probation officer and copied in to me. It outlined the struggle that she has to accommodate people coming to the Rock on a regular basis whilst still getting them to comply with the other terms of their orders. She also expressed worries that offenders were being pressurised to attend in order to appease me, the film crew or Rocky. She points out that after our conversation she realises that I do not really understand what an order involves.

Her solution is to have more people attending for less time – ideally one day a week. This would not infringe on the rest of the order and would maximise the benefits of what we are offering at the Rock. Her email went on to point out that there was an almost total lack of communication within the service as to what we are doing and how we are doing it.

I replied:

Thanks for sending the attachment through. I am sorry that I could not respond sooner but I have been abroad filming.

There are a number of good and important points that you raise in your letter and whilst I would love the opportunity to meet soon and discuss them at length, I will just pick up on a couple now.

The project has three key strands.

1. That it involves offenders working within their local area, climate and community. This means that they connect directly to the society that they live in.

2. That they raise produce that goes directly back into that community. In other words they share the fruits of their work. Nothing is anonymous. Everyone and everything is directly accountable.

3. Eating local, organic food, ideally raised by them, at a communal table is the single most important aspect. Nothing else will change behaviour more effectively.

As to their attendance, there are two pieces of empirical evidence that support a broader assumption.

1. The more days that they attend in any week the more beneficial it is. 5 days would be best.
2. There has to be regular attendance with not less than 7 days between visits and preferably 3 days.

Both these factors make a huge difference to their behaviour and states of mind. One day a week is only just worthwhile and is certainly not a model. Two days should be the minimum and three days the desired goal.

I think that there is a general mutual lack of comprehension. It is true that I have no knowledge or interest in the bureaucracy of the probation service or courts but of one thing I am clear: The project is *not* just part of an order. It is a self-contained entity that hopefully can work alongside orders or any other nomenclature of offenders. At the moment it is operating within orders but in many ways the orders hinder the work of the project as much as they help it. Yet I fully appreciate that without the existing – and entirely noble – work of the probation service we would not be in existence.

In other words I see the project as an alternative to what is being done at the moment. The fact that it is rooted in the soil and growing edible products and caring for livestock is the *essence* of it. It is NOT just a way of 'filling their time' (a phrase that I found deeply depressing).

I have set up a charitable foundation to pursue this. Obviously we wish to work with the probation service in every detail and with absolute cooperation. But I do NOT see it as a sideline. It is right at the heart of how I believe we can help offenders – particularly those addicted to drugs.

However, I am the first to admit that its goals are modest. I think that groups of 6–10 are the optimum size. It would not be appropriate for many offenders. It is deliberately local, parochial and low key. The beauty of it is that it is infinitely reproducible. Lots of small successes can change big things.

So to increase the opportunities for more people it is necessary to increase the number of projects rather than reducing the number of days that people spend there. Without exception all the feedback that I have had is that they would all like to spend more days on the project rather than less.

As for Andrés, I would not feel that we had succeeded with him until a) he has a proper job and b) he is drug free. At the moment he is as addicted to methadone as he is to heroin and alcohol. Although he is amazingly impressive he is also incredibly fragile. It would not surprise me at all if he was to go backwards into heavy drug use.

I am wholly sympathetic and frustrated with your lack of briefing. I suspect that it is endemic within all government bureaucracies but clearly it has to change. However, the human communication – between Rocky, David Chantler, the Trust members, the BBC etc. – is very good. That has to be organised so that it can function smoothly and efficiently.

At the moment no one is running the project. No one. It is a muddle between Rocky, myself and David. I actually see this as a tribute to the essential simplicity of it, but it is not sustainable. From the outset I have wanted a fully dedicated probation officer whose sole job is to organise this and any other sites within the area. They would coordinate every aspect of delivery to the sites of offenders, carers and budget. If finance is a problem it may be that my charity can help – although I would strongly argue that such a post is almost instantly cost-efficient. But at the moment we are muddling through on a wing and a prayer. In practice it means that I am providing large chunks of finance and time. This inevitably makes me proprietorial – hence the tone of this email!

What we are doing at the Rock is a blueprint. We are learning daily on how to go about this. You cannot underestimate the effect that the filming has on this process. The nation will be scrutinising every aspect and if it works we can create a huge change. In other words it is wholly wrong to treat this as part of an existing system.

Everything has to be rethought and reworked. The only way to do that successfully is by tapping into the knowledge and experience of probation workers. We need to work together on this but outside existing paradigms. People like you are doing heroic and unacknowledged work day in and day out. Rather than sweep in and bypass that in a flurry of TV and ego, I want to do what I can – and I know that it is minuscule – to help. I want to do this for the long term.

So – lots to talk about.

Yours

Monty Don

I never had a reply to my email and have had no more communication about this matter from the probation officer – who, it should be stressed, is clearly a conscientious, over-worked, entirely professional person trying to do the best that she can. Without their support, working on the ground and managing the practicalities of the orders with the offenders with huge pressures and inadequate resources, the project will inevitably struggle.

I went in to the Rock, where Andrés, Paul and Chubby were already there, driven by Tony. Rocky rang to say that he was still in Worcester as Chris – a new bloke – couldn't get his script until lunchtime. The chemist had apparently run out of methadone over the bank holiday. Given that bank holidays are announced in the average desk diary at least nine months ahead, you might have thought that such things were catered for. Anyway, Chris was left at home to rattle and Rocky arrived later with just Kate.

I asked Andrés if he only stayed three days a week to please me, Rocky or the BBC. He looked aghast and panicked.

I'd come five days a week if I could he said.

What about the Cathedral and National Trust jobs?

They haven't even answered my letters. I'd love to do that – two days a week – which would still mean I could come here three or even five days. What would I do on the day I wasn't here? Have a couple of drinks, go into town, be bored, score a bag to ease the boredom, good day out.

He was being ironic but not a trace of a smile. For the rest of the day his body slumped. I have never met anyone whose body language was so indicative of state of mind or responsive to situations.

I asked Chubby about being caught in possession of speed.

Bit of a cunt Mont, he said.

You certainly are I said. Any luck with jobs?

I rang twelve people yesterday and nothing.

Being caught again in possession isn't going to help I said.

You're right. I got to avoid them situations.

He seemed contrite and pissed off. I learned later that he had raging toothache. Go to a dentist I said.

Haven't got one Mont. I've used up my free dental credit. I've got some pliers at home. I'll pull the bastard.

My mind full of the potential conflict with the probation service about how to go about the project, we talked about continuity and what they were gaining. The consensus was that building a team was the thing, making something and seeing it through. You could not do that on one day a week and hardly on two. The more they put in the more they got out.

Ha.

Maurice the Wood came and took them off to gather bean sticks from Wigmore Rolls. I said I would wait for Kate and Rocky and come later. In fact Kate did not want to go so we stayed behind and transplanted Super Marmande tomatoes that had been put into the tunnel outside into a raised bed. (The tomatoes had fabulous roots on them. When I rang Andy Trim later and happened to mention this he said Ah that will be the biodynamic preps. I want to scoff and mock this but who knows? Everyone who has ever used biodynamic methods invariably comments on the astonishing results.)

As Kate and I planted in that big open field she told me about her childhood.

She is having counselling but says that it's no fucking use.

All they do is sit there saying Right, right. I understand. How does that make you *feel*? Fucking wankers. I want advice not asking me how I *feel*. Not fucking great. I've given up blubbing and crying whenever I talk about it. I did mind. Not now. I want help now.

We continue to plant tomatoes.

Rocky left early with Kate and Chubby as they had a doctor's appointment to go to. Paul, Andrés and Tony remain, earthing up potatoes. I planted squashes and courgettes that I had grown at home. The sun shone. Trees laden with glowing green. Despite the lingering resonance of Kate's misery, it was a strangely happy hour or so.

Kate Hirschfield

I'm twenty-six. I was born on 18 March 1980 in Ronkswood Hospital, Worcester. I'm the youngest of four children – well, my mum had a daughter before she met my dad then two sons and a daughter before she had me.

My dad was from Worcester and his dad. Actually the family came from Germany. It's really spelt without an 'i' – Hirschfeld.

Dad left Mum when I was about six or seven months I think. Or Mum left Dad. The social services split us up. Me and my next brother went into care and the oldest two went to foster homes. I went to a family in Dines Green, Worcester. They were my mum and dad, that's what I thought – know what I mean? Then when I was four the social services stuck two big cardboard boxes of my stuff in the boot and took me away to my dad. I was shocked. Didn't speak to my dad for a week. I still see the foster family. They say that they've failed me – bit disappointed really. But I tell them that they haven't.

My dad had a partner with two children but we were always rowing. Then they split up. When I was six and a half my dad got the partner he's with now. I like her. My dad's father and my nan lived down the road.

I liked primary school. Yeah, enjoyed it. Kept my head down. Then I went to Christopher Whitehead School in St John's Worcester. The first day I got knocked out when a wooden ball hit me. I'd only been there ten minutes. I got picked on at first.

Between eleven and thirteen I was a loner at school. Then at thirteen I tried to kill myself. Paracetamol. I left a note. Woke up three days later with tubes and couldn't speak. That scared Dad.

I was picked on until fifth year then stood up for meself. Started using cannabis and speed when I was about thirteen, with other people. I took GCSEs and got five with C or above. Then in 1996 I left school and went to Worcester Technical College studying childcare.

I had an evening job at Kays and used the money for recreational drugs. At sixteen I had a boyfriend who used speed and smack but I never. I didn't really understand it.

When I was seventeen I had this big argument with Dad because we went on holiday and I slept with this married man. Only he didn't know that. He thought I was just out late. Dad went mad at me because I had gone missing for three hours.

I started using gear around then, while I was still at the Tech. My dealer said the only way I could use it was to inject so I never smoked it. I didn't mind the injections. It made me sick as soon as I used but I liked it because I didn't think about anything. I weren't bothered by anything. Just wanted to kill all the pain. I used for three months then stopped for nine months.

I met my mum when I was seventeen – just before I started using. She was living in Wolverhampton with my half-brothers and half-sister, living with this big Rasta man. He's a good bloke.

I phone her. Keep in touch.

Then on 12 August 1998 I met my boyfriend. I was eighteen. He had just got out of jail that day. I had no criminal record up to then. But we just started nicking all the time.

I started using crack in 1998. It was nice. Nice! It's just a dark, moody drug you didn't tell people about. But it makes you offend more. I was a bad crack addict when I first came here. Gear and crack walk together. Crack to get you up and gear to come down. I was sick every time I used gear and crack for two years. That's what gave me my stomach trouble. Two seconds after a hit I would go greugh and be sick. But I liked the feeling after I was sick. In 2000 I was rushed to hospital. I had been in bed for a month. I couldn't hold any food down. My boyfriend said I was faking so I didn't have to go shoplifting – but he used to have to carry me to the toilet.

We had some good times but it was just a drug relationship. I stayed with him till 2003. Dad hates him. Absolutely hates him.

In 2000 I got a caution. In 2001 I went to prison for possession with intent to supply. I didn't like being locked up but kept my head down. I've been to prison four times but I never took drugs in prison. Well I would if someone brought me something when they visited but I never went and looked for any or bought any.

In 2004 I was clean for nine months. I stayed clean because I met a girl. My boyfriend says it was bad enough me dumping him but for a girl! It was my first proper girlfriend. Then she was going to join the Ministry of Defence and they said that she shouldn't be with me. We had rows about it and she was put off. I went straight back on gear when she finished with me.

In 2004 I went to jail on remand for two months for shoplifting and dizzy driving – driving without documents, insurance or that and then I got two years DTTO for that offence which is what I am doing now.

I went to a party on Saturday and all my mates were there from when I was sixteen. They were all really chuffed to see me and saying I was doing well. It was nice to be with people who didn't want something, who weren't with you just because they were after gear or some money. They were just being friendly.

I'd like to get married and have kids and have a normal life. It isn't much to ask for is it?

June 2006

4/6/06

Driving back from a day of bracken cutting – long, hot and completely happy – I get a message from Butch, the BBC director for the past six months, saying that he won't be working on the project anymore. This is bad news for me and all the group as he has had a paternal presence and entirely benign influence over the whole place. They adore him in particular and as ever, hate change in general.

5/6/06

Spend too much time filming an insert to go with stuff shot last spring (fifteen months ago). As all the retakes and minute additions take place I can hear the group going about our business and listening anxiously. It feels as though I am moon-lighting.

Kate reacts powerfully when she learns that Butch is not to return due to ill health – a safe paternal figure lost. Tears and anger.

That's it she says. Fuck 'em. I'll only film with Butch. I don't want no other poncy cunt. They can get Butch back or I'll fuck off.

But there is not a hint of intent in her voice. The only way she can express regret is with threat and anger.

The tunnels have not been watered over the weekend and trays of seedlings are burned up. It is almost vandalism. Fucking cunts Kate says. At least she cares. Paul says that he will definitely come in over the weekend from now on and I agree to cover his wages. The probation service has been painfully slow over this – our shrivelled plants are the result.

Tony goes off to get pig feed and hose fittings and comes back cross and late having gone to the wrong place. It takes another trip after lunch to get the pig feed. Everything is clumsy today. Everything jarring. Andy Trim is there and a muscular, busy presence amongst their wanness. But at least they are all busy.

Andy B says he feels really drugged today. Doesn't know why. He is injecting himself with ampoules of methadone in his cunning plan to stop using. The net effect is to give him a massive dose of methadone – his 90 ml script plus the 40 odd ml intravenously. He has the stains under his eyes of a user in bad nick. But he drives the tractor expertly and is really very good at it despite being really very drugged. We walk into lunch. I say that we must keep the place tidy for the open day. What you'd like to see is me with a broomstick up my arse he says. Coming from Andy, this is not as completely surprising as it might otherwise be.

Broomsticks could be good I say but not sure about the arse bit.

Well that's what the birds like he said.

Uh?

They love it, they do. He nodded solemnly. It's true.

And he went off to have his bacon sandwich.

Complaints at lunch because I had bought chicken and mushroom pies again. In practice they have probably had this once a fortnight for the past three months.

We can't eat like this Monty, Kate said. We need variety. We need potatoes and things.

Don't know whether to be delighted or outraged. At least there is an expression of active interest in food. But we pick our first harvest of broad beans and have them along with the pies and a salad for lunch. Andy Trim says we can't pick them this small.

Got to I say. They are nicer small.

You'll never sell them like this in Herefordshire he says. They like them the bigger the better. It's more value for money and if you are selling them by the pound you need a few pods. You've got to be posh to eat them like this.

Well I am food-posh. And so should we be on the project. Posh and proud of it. Kate has just one bean and says she doesn't like it and Paul, Andy B and Tony refuse to try them. But they are undeniably good.

Kate has tears in her eyes all lunchtime because of Butch's going. Everyone feels bad about it too. A family member has gone.

Rocky tells me about the site that he and David Chantler went to visit last week, just a few miles outside Worcester. It is apparently perfect and has huge possibilities. Rocky, as ever, is cagey about saying too much but clearly excited by it. It would transform his working life, being right in the heart of his group.

But I realise that he would see this as a direct extension or translocation of this group and site. In fact it is hardly likely to be the case. Nothing at the Rock belongs to this group. It is of the place and the project. So the new site would have to start again with a completely new infrastructure. I am sure Rocky has not thought of this, nor of the extra financing needed. I suspect that he imagines the whole thing would move lock, stock and barrel to the new, undeniably more convenient for this group, site. I must talk to him about all this.

On top of this Andy Trim is advising on keeping the Rock whatever – if only as a base for growing things and keeping animals to stock other sites. It would be a way of keeping the commercial and trading side going whilst new sites got built up. The rent would therefore be more than covered and some of the set-up costs recouped. There is a powerful logic to this and would remain handy for me and him.

I see difficult discussions ahead.

05.06.06

Sunny day, loads of work done. We still have loads of work to do. Enjoyed myself.

Andrés Pope

Hello everyone. I'm back! My birthday is on 11 June and what a day. Fuckin hell it's bloody hot!!

Andy B

After the others left I stayed and chatted to Paul before giving him a lift home. This is Paul's story.

Paul Mellor

I was born on 7 July 1979 in Croxteth, Liverpool. My family are all scousers. I was the youngest of eight children. I can't remember anything about Liverpool. My dad got a job in Leominster when I was seven and we have been in my current house since then. My mum worked as a residential social worker looking after disabled people. Dad was area manager for Provident Personal Credit.

I went to Leominster Primary School. Don't remember much about it but I do remember the end because I was split up from my mates who went to the local Minster School. The Minster wouldn't accept me because of what my brother had been like. He had been in all sorts of trouble. So they didn't want me.

I went to Wigmore School. I enjoyed it. It's a really good

school. I was successful at school. Nine GCSEs and captain of all sports. I left school and went to a YTS day centre for the disabled working for my NVQ level 2. I worked really hard for eighteen months on £45 a week and had done all the written work but when they came to the oral stuff the examiners went to the wrong building. They told me that I would have to start all over again. That's when it all started to go wrong.

The same day my dad got me a job as a print assistant on nearly £300 a week.

I started clubbing, getting into drugs – cannabis, speed, ecstasy, acid. But just at weekends and paid for out of the money I was earning. I was going round with my brother and his mates. He is five years older than me. The next one up. None of my other brothers or sisters was into drugs or crime though.

People with my brother were using class A drugs but no one dared offer me heroin when he was around. He was into speed. That was his thing. But not heroin. I was partying at weekends and holding the job down.

Then one night I was supposed to go clubbing with my brother but was asked to stay behind at home with one of his supposed best mates. My brother went off and immediately the heroin came out. I tried it of course. Smoked it. I liked it straight away. I was sick of course – everyone is sick when they first use – but – I liked that feeling, like I had no care in the world.

This friend of my brother's said to me that night What would you do if you were down to your last ten quid now? And I said I'd go and get some more heroin. That was the very first time. It was a spiral from that first go. Next morning I had to get some more. I was an addict within two or three months spending every penny of my wage packet on it.

My brother went mad, had a fight with the dealer who supplied it. Went mad he did.

I started injecting when I was about eighteen or nineteen. I couldn't afford to keep going smoking £300 a week. When you smoke heroin you always waste some. Some gets left on the foil after you gouge out and drift off. When you inject you get *everything*. Nothing is wasted. I think that injecting is for the people that want to do it in private. Smoking is for the people who have been clubbing and smoke to come down off the ecstasy in the morning.

The job went after I started injecting. The cluck (cold turkey) is stronger when you are injecting. I couldn't work and not use. My dad fired me. He knew all along. At the time I didn't care. I didn't care about anything except the next hit. I never had any problems with injecting. No trouble with it at all.

I would go to Gloucester or Birmingham to score. I had been hanging round with my brother's friends. They all dressed smartly, holding down jobs. Then I started mixing with other, lower levels.

I was nineteen when I got into trouble with the law for the first time. Caught in possession with intent to supply. I was using an eighth and teenth (16th) a day by then (4.75 grams – over 20 bags @ £10 each). I was caught with ten bags and got two and a half years in jail. I went to Bristol Young Offenders unit. I felt terrified. I got my head knocked in by six people on the third day. Young Offenders are terrible places. Everybody wants to be Jack-the-lad. Adult prisons are easy. Everyone just wants to get by. I've had a fair few beatings. I survived by locking myself in my cell for three months. I was lucky cos I shared a cell with a local lad from Hereford.

I did fifteen months and was clean all the way through but I was back on gear after one week of being let out. They give you a wodge of money – discharge grant and 50 per cent of your fortnightly giro and community care grant. You think great – I'll see so and so and have a drink and do this – and one thing leads to another. When you get out and you've been clean all that time you don't think that's it, I'll stay clean. Something makes you think I'll just do one bag – just get that feeling again.

I never minded using. The thing I minded most was not wearing a T-shirt in hot weather. You can spot the users on a summer's day. They've all got long sleeves and trousers.

Six months later I was in jail again for burglary. My next door neighbour's house. Another two and a half years. I never used in jail. I would do education. Business studies. Sociology.

All this time I lived at home and my parents still visited me every week. Still gave me money. Still wrote to me. When I came out I met a girl and stayed clean for two years. Dad got me my job back at the printers. I was twenty-two/twenty-three. Then we broke up and did gear the next day. Two months later I was caught thieving and was given a drug testing and treatment order. But I breached custody and escaped from a police car. Went on the run. I got nine months for that.

Came out – did well, stayed off for a good few months. Then same old thing. Back on gear. Second DTTO, which was this one. By now I was getting tired of it. Sick of it all. Started passing tests, playing football. I had four months of negatives. But last Christmas I was doing crack again. Going to Gloucester four times a day – bus, train, car – anything. Gloucester is a big drug centre. I spent all of Mum and Dad's money over Christmas. They bulk up the giros before Christmas and it all went. I had to tell my parents that I had spent all their money on drugs. It was the first time that I admitted it. They started going with me everywhere. If I had to get a bus they would come with me and see me on it so I wouldn't give in to temptation. They were helping me.

Then I came here. I nearly didn't come. I had £12 and needed £3 to score and was about to leave when Rocky rang to say he was just down the road. I enjoyed it right from the off, me. I was desperate for something like this I think.

I don't speak to all but one of my brothers and sisters. Only Graham who is the straightest one of the lot. Ex-army. They all cut me out. To be honest I've got no problem if I never saw them again. But even Graham would never have me in the house because of the drugs. He's got kids. Now I'm clean I go and help him put up a shed and that. We go to the pub together.

I need to get out into the community and get clean. Clean from methadone as well as gear. I'm not out of that lifestyle yet. I still have to collect my methadone with all the other users. By Christmas I'll be clean. My dream is to spend Christmas day clean with my family.

I still smoke ganj but that's £30 a week I can't afford. That will have to go too. But for the moment I don't touch it till after my tea, when I know I've done everything I've got to do and then that's my time.

I want to know that this place will continue. To have my own flat. A girlfriend. Pass my driving test and have a car or a bike. To be normal.

My worst fear is my mum seeing me back on gear.

6/6/06

6/6/6. Mark of the beast. Only Paul, Andrés, and a new person, Chris, come. Chris is slight, pale and has a nice smile. He tells me he is on a script of 60 ml. Is that OK? I ask.

It'll hold me till this evening like.

Then will you use?

Yeah.

Ah well. At least we start out honest about this. We set him to watering and find him a little later sitting on the tractor. I had forgotten that back last summer they were all like this. They would do ten or fifteen minutes and then disappear to sit down or go back to the mess room. Their stamina and concentration levels were nil. At times the whole group would dissipate and much of my time was spent like a scout master trying to encourage them with a rather hearty team spirit. Now I rarely have to think about that. We just do stuff.

I have to go at midday to drive down to Sissinghurst. It is a hot day and a long drive – five hours without break, and takes me from one world to another as far removed as can probably be imagined. It is also the longest time that Sarah and I have had together, other than when asleep, for over a fortnight.

7/6/06

I go to London early with a hangover to record 'Desert Island Discs' for Radio 4 and to meet my publisher. Dan and Adam, who have been filming the project for over a year now, plus a sound recordist, meet me at Broadcasting House to film all this. I choose Nick Drake's 'Road' for the project but Sue Lawley does not pick up on it and it is scarcely talked about. She is much more interested in talking about my depression. I feel phoney about this. Perhaps she feels it too because she refers a number of times to my happy smiling face. The truth is I hate talking about depression. I honestly feel as though I know nothing. I am still not sure whether I am not just supremely self-centred and gloomy and that bucking up, pulling my socks up or getting on with it – make up your own brisk phrase – would not do the trick.

The crew comment on how great the girls look in the London sun. Adam points out that he has spent so long with the group that he takes their thinness and general shambling aura of ill-health as a kind of norm. To come to a prosperous city where the body-beautiful is assiduously cultivated and celebrated is a shock. But a lovely one.

We look at pictures whilst at the publishers taken last September when the team of horses came to plough. Kate is impossibly thin, Wayne and Lee there – both now in prison. Andrés ghostly. Tom wonderfully photogenic in a way that is completely surprising. I think of the scratched and raw face after his crack binges and the fidgeting irritation with everybody and everything. You would never know the troubles beneath that skin from the photographs.

12/6/06

Visited the farm shop down the road and got incredibly positive reception. Basically they will take any vegetables that we can grow and in return we will barter meat or whatever they have excess of. This suits us fine and is a huge step forward in both local acceptance and a practical outlet. Fiona's husband would also apparently be happy to instruct and help us with sheep. Again a real process of integration and acceptance.

Got to the Rock by 10.30, worried that they would have got there before me. Fat chance. In the end no one turned up before 11.30 and did not get going with anything before midday. Apparently Tony's car broke down. The truth is that the whole focus of their attention is on getting there. Just doing that is target enough whereas I think in terms of what we have to do. There is almost an inverse correlation between their urgency and when they arrive. The later they are the more reluctant they seem to be to get cracking. Some of this is doubtless due to the long car journey, but I know the syndrome myself. After a certain point hurry seems irrelevant.

David and Tricia were having new carpets fitted. One of the fitters came out of the door and saw the crew with wide-mouthed amazement. What are they doing? My real reaction was equally surprised – what are YOU doing on our patch? But I just smiled. You're Monty aren't you? Yup. My girlfriend says you live round here but I said you never. She'll be chuffed that she's right.

Find Andy Trim. He is keen that we stay there so we don't waste the set-up that has been laboriously established. I think that we could but would have to completely renegotiate the relationship with our landlords. Both parties need more separation and autonomy within clearly defined areas. The Reeves are kind, very decent people but have found it hard to accommodate the chaos of this project.

When they do finally get to the farm – Kate, Paul, Andrés, Dean, Chris Smith, and – much later – Andy B with the broken-down Tony – I get them weeding, planting and tying tomatoes. Then immediately a meeting with Marsha, Rocky, Andy Trim and David Chantler to discuss sites. Rocky wants to set up a new site near Worcester and had assumed that this would simply mean relocating the project. To him it is solely him and his group. To me he is one element in a much bigger picture, albeit at the moment the most important one. This means that he assumes that all the gear and fittings would go with him. It raises the important question of who owns the assets. David Chantler makes a number of things clear:

1. He can only support Rocky in Worcester and will guarantee finance for it.
2. He had not considered staying at the Rock as an option.
3. He would like to set up a project venture in Herefordshire, Worcester and Shropshire but does not feel that he can instigate or manage that now. One is all he can engage with and that would have to be Rocky's.
4. He would like the charity to set up a central base that owned the assets of sites, engaged managers and co-ordinated everything but the offenders and their management.
5. He would support staying at the Rock and help with a team from Hereford as long as we arranged the manager.

Andy Trim argued that the cost of moving the physical set-up would almost be as great as starting from scratch and that the pros far outweighed the cons of this site. Also the integration with the local community was a slow and hard-won thing. To leave after one year would be seen as a failure. David agreed with all that but thought that this might be inevitable.

In the end we all agreed that it was up to me to sort out the charity as soon as possible. I made it clear that my involvement with Rocky's group would cease to be personal when he moved, but that I would help as I could. David made the point – when Rocky had gone – that Rocky would follow the project's guide but if we did not come up with clear agricultural and ideological guidelines then he would inevitably do his own thing. That would not necessarily be a bad thing but it would be certain.

Kate and Andrés were disgruntled that Paul now has a paid job, tending the site on the three days that no one is here and working down at the farm shop. Andrés was uncharacteristically quiet – and his quietness is of a wan, withheld quality that I have rarely come across before. It resonates. I suspect that they feel left out, that something else has passed them by. But I did not have a chance to talk to them about this. Did not have a chance to talk much to any of them. Too much filming and too much of a photographer taking pictures for BBC publicity.

Kate said that she despised herself for being on telly and speaking to the camera. Some of the fucking things I've said. They can't show them. I've asked them to show me it before it goes out. They can't show them.

I suspect that the reality of this appearing is beginning to seep in. Also the reality that she is still a junkie, no job and not a lot of hope. At lunch I called Chris a stupid fucker and Kate immediately jumped on that.

You're always saying things like that to us. It's not right. Stupid fucked up junkies. You shouldn't say these things.

I said that I tried to tell the truth.

But that's just *rude*.

She was right. So I apologised.

Chris showed me his leg – swollen, white flesh with a mass of black abscesses, ulcers and bruises from the needles. I asked him to show the camera. He adamantly refused.

No way man. That's gross. My family would kill me if they saw that, man.

He has a nice face and manner. Big smile. Doesn't say much. He uses ten bags a day 'and the crack too'. He is twenty-five and lives at home with his mum. I asked what she thought of him using.

She hates it man. Hates it. He smiles when he says this – says almost anything – sweet and rueful at the same time. I bet his mum does hate it, more than anything else in the world.

We planted out chard seedlings and did a lot of watering. Kate picked broad beans for the shop and Andy B weeded all the seed beds. I had a long chat with him after the others had all gone except him and Rocky. It was his birthday yesterday he said, twenty-seven I think, and I asked about the coming year.

Don't suppose I'll live to be twenty-eight. Really?

Nah. I was joking.

He can play the junkie game pretty well. His aunt, brother and cousin have all been users. Andy is the only one still addicted. His cousin is dead.

I only started using so I wouldn't care what people said. I was so high I took no notice. I want to get myself sorted now. It's time. Get my hearing aid. Get off gear. But it's not the getting off that's hard. It's staying away from it. All the dealers and users and people. I went to the pub the other day and everyone was taking pills and drinking but I didn't like it.

I went to a wedding at the weekend and had a really nice time. Drank Jack Daniels and Coke and homemade cider. Got wasted and woke up with no head at all. That was good. I had a brilliant time. Down the pub six girls tried to take my trousers off. Me dad had me head in an arm lock like this (he held an imaginary head under the crook of his arm) and the girls tried to take me trousers down. Interesting. The truth is I don't like drinking. I has to force myself.

I don't know what I want to do. Ten years ago I didn't know what I wanted to do. I still don't. All that learning all those skills and I don't know what to do with them. I thought of going on an oil rig – four weeks on and two weeks off. No chance of using on the rig. But they wouldn't just take me on, hand me a lump of metal and say get on with it. But it would do me good. Four weeks on and two weeks off. I wouldn't use then.

He speaks with great certainty and assurance in unconnected phrases that often have an internal logic. His life is lived almost entirely in his head – but with quite a lot of order.

19/6/06

Meeting with David and Tricia about future of the Rock. They surprised me by offering the possibility of a three-year lease. Also by accepting my proposal of the project taking whole of backyard and relinquishing any of the inner yard so that they would have a buffer zone between them and us to try and establish measurable, easily recognisable demarcation lines.

If we take it I would have to underwrite the rent. I would also have to find a manager. There is also the possibility that the Trust/probation service could take all the infrastructure (although this would be barmy and is a bit unlikely).

Only Kate, Chris and Andy B turned up. Andrés's mother's flat had flooded so he had to attend to that, Chubby has a job for a week, Paul is now off on Monday, Tuesday and Wednesday and the others were unavailable. We got them weeding and planting but it was slow.

We talked about the open day, which is only a week away, but Andy B is hinting at not coming, although he won't say why.

> On the 21st we are having a OPEN Day I feel like not coming because I'm not very good meeting people! I hate it I really do?! I coming tomorrow.
>
> Andy B

20/6/06

I spent much time trying to fix my ride-on mower the night before and early in the morning and went into shop for lunch, a socket set and 125 bamboo canes at 8.30. Hired a trailer and loaded it up with ride-on mower, strimmer and rakes etc. The idea was to tidy as much as poss before the open day.

Ride-on broke almost immediately and took a couple of hours fiddling to fix. As we were doing so the pig suddenly appeared at our shoulder with three piglets in tow. She was friendly and interested but reluctant to be caught. Finally snatched a piglet – which screeched incessantly – and she anxiously followed me back to their section of the brook and wood to look after it.

Chris spilt his methadone in his pocket – didn't put the cap on properly – so by three was rattling. I asked him what he was going to do.

Score as soon as I can.

Did he have any money?

No.

So what will you do? I knew the answer of course.

Go thieving.

That's not good.

I know. But I gotta. There's no other way. He shook his head, genuinely rueful.

I hope he comes in tomorrow.

Early in the day, over lunch (as Chris was recovering from the shock of finding a hair in his sandwich – at which point he refused to eat anything else. I pointed out the incongruity of that from someone who admitted shooting up. But the needles are clean, he said. They never have hairs in them) he said, I like woods, me.

Oh yeah? Do you like coppicing?

No. I like playing in the woods. When I was a kid we played all day in the woods, messing about, making camps, tracking. I really like the woods me.

Heroin takes the woods away from you. Locks you in empty rooms.

Kate was almost unable to walk and spent most of the day with her bandaged leg up. It was black with internal bleeding. She says the nurses do nothing.

It hurts like fuck I tell them. They come back with It can't hurt cos you're on heroin.

What will happen Kate?

She brightens up on the medical detail. They going to strip the veins to see if that helps. If that don't work they'll take the leg off.

That sounds pretty bad I say.

Nah. I want it. I know loads of people who've had their leg amputated. It would sort it out.

Chris had two abscesses on his arm. I asked how. He said that he had let a friend shoot up for him – and I paid him to – and that he had butchered me. Were the needles clean I asked. Oh yes. Always clean needles he said. Despite this he mowed almost everything with the push mower.

We staked all the tomatoes, planted out sunflowers, sweet peas, pak choi and lettuce, cut grass, watered, weeded and generally tidied.

I came home at five astonishingly tired although on any other kind of work I would be good for another two or three hours. I unload all the equipment and put it away, have a cup of tea then go and garden for a few hours. England are playing football. I can hear it coming from the neighbours' tellys. I rake up cut grass and plant out Little Gem Lettuce.

21/6/06 Open Day

The longest day.

Went first to Leominster to Paul's house to pick him and a barbecue up. There was a big Sold sign up outside the house. Paul wasn't there, gone to the bank, but his dad helped me load up a very fancy gas barbecue. He's done really well I said. You must be proud of him.

I am he said, a gentle northern voice. Slippers. A lot of that's down to you he said. No it isn't I said, it's down to Paul.

He wasn't going to come that first day you know. It was his mother that said give it a go. Just for one day. And he's never looked back.

I see you've sold, I said.

Yes. We've had enough. We've got a boat being built. He beamed.

Sailing away.

On to the Rock with no one there but Marsha followed me in and we unloaded the gear. Found Beth feeding the pigs. Our paths have hardly crossed but she is young, cheery, energetic and full of life. A kind of attractive goal for them to aim at with their frailty and decrepitude. She and Andy Trim make a good balancing team although they are an unlikely combination.

The team arrived in dribs and drabs with Rocky and Jack bringing their wives who immediately added an aura of busy competence to the place. We need more women on the scheme. It feels much better like that.

The *Hereford Times* arrived with reporter and photographer at eleven and I showed them round, and posed for pictures. Then television news, who were, it seems a little more cynical, asking the guys if I ever did any work or just came along occasionally and told them what to do. I feel surprisingly unperturbed about this. I don't care. The general assumption of honesty inures one to this kind of thing and is amazingly strengthening. Then Radio Hereford and Worcester came and stayed a long time, chatting to everyone.

All this created a kind of buzz that was new to the site – people were coming to regard us and seemed to like what they saw, which was a pretty novel experience.

We broke for lunch after tidying, weeding, raking and generally preening and the first visitors started arriving at two and kept flowing in all afternoon until about 7 p.m. We had magistrates, police chiefs, Trust members, neighbours and above all, families of the group.

Kate's father and brother came, much to her high anxiety and excitement. She had told us that he had initially said that he would definitely not come. That it was too far. Who was going to pay for the petrol? It was the wrong time. She is like a little girl with her father, desperate to please. She changed twice in the morning and had her hair done for him. I had imagined an elderly figure but in fact he was not much older than me. Her brother was more tattoo than flesh and shook my hand with the characteristic action of most of the new offenders – limp hand and head turned away.

These family tableaux were incredibly interesting and illuminating. Dean's parents came from Chippenham and his girlfriend and son – almost as tall as Dean. Dean's mother obviously a bit bewildered by his drug use – Were you using both the drugs son? (meaning I think both methadone and heroin) and Why did you lie to me son? To his eternal credit Dean looked embarrassed. I didn't want to upset you he said. We're not mugs son, his dad said. It was as touching a moment as I saw all day.

Andrés's mother said she had found her son again after twenty years. He was, she said, the last person in the world that she thought would go out and work in the mud and the rain. I told her that he was the first to do such things here.

The overall expressions from the families was one of surprise.

Martin's parents came. Martin's tree looks horribly like it is dying – from drought I think. I hope to God they didn't go up and look too closely. They stayed a long time. I asked how she was. I'm all right she said. Getting on. We've moved. Couldn't stay there any longer. Got a smaller house now. Big garden though.

Chris (who couldn't do any physical work because the abscess on his arm was bad) drove the tractor, doing the compost and lining up the machinery to look good. At one point he was tooting the horn and mucking about with Andy B clinging onto the back. They were both alike, baseball caps, preternaturally skinny and rotten mouthed. I warned them that a group of magistrates had arrived and that he should be on his best behaviour. Not fucking magistrates! he said, genuinely aghast (despite the fact that we had told them all clearly). I hate fucking magistrates and they fucking hates me. No they don't I said. They're just doing a job.

Not with me they ain't. They fucking loves putting me away.

Poor you I said. Don't be so self pitying. Keep out of trouble and you won't go to prison.

I can't 'cause I can't get a job and with no job I got to thieve haven't I?

Nope. You could stop using.

Yeah! (said in a tone of incredulity)

Stop using and get a job.

No one will give me one will they.

Stop using and we will help you get a job. Stop being so sorry for yourself. Come here as often as you can. We will get you clean and then get you a job – I almost believed myself.

I want a job. I want to work as a labourer for you.

Anyway I went and spoke to a group of magistrates arriving like very self-confident hikers with boots and sticks out for a stroll and lunch in a jolly nice little pub. I pointed out Chris and Andy. Oh yes I know those two said one. I've put them away more than once. We all laughed. But half an hour later I saw the same person being shown around by Chris, the two shoulder to shoulder.

Kate said that she had been picking spinach with a police superintendent (impossibly crisp and clean white shirt, gym-honed jawline). She said to him, I normally don't like cunts like you but you're all right.

It was a topsy-turvy day almost drunk with its own success.

We cooked and served 200 of Tudges' sausages (made a few miles up the road) and probably half as many again of our own, 100 free range local chicken legs and breast, rolls, and kebabs. Kate came to find me before her family arrived, shouting: Monty! we need peppers for the kebabs! Send Marsha to buy some! It's not the season Kate. I don't fucking care. You can't have kebabs without red in them. Lots of tea was drunk. None of this by me as I did not have a moment to eat or drink. Home by 8.30.

It felt like a conclusion. Like suddenly finding yourself on the brow of a hill that you have been slogging up without any real expectation of conquering.

Two things:

1. We have to stay at the Rock. It would be an undoing to leave now. More would be lost than gained.
2. I have to really push with the charity to enable the funding to be sorted.

David Chantler told me that the total costs for this year probably amounted to 150k. I am sure that this could be reduced to 125k with control and care. It includes set-up costs that would amortise across five years. The running costs are probably about 100k a year. This would process about 10 people. So 10k–15k per person compared to 35k per person in jail – and we teach them something, heal them and have a real chance of rehabilitation.

22/6/06

The *Hereford Times* gave us its front cover and all its editorial space and was uncritically supportive. Good piece on TV news last night too but the local press is more important and one decent piece there is worth ten in the national press.

Picked up HIT leaflet, glossy, bright pink, pocket sized, that had been left in the mess room for the open day. Presumably this is dished out to all users on a script. It is eminently practical and sensible and completely uncensorious in its tone.

METHADONE AND SAFETY Staying Alive
Methadone is a potentially dangerous drug. Here are some golden rules to help you stay alive.

Don't Use Methadone With Other Drugs
Using methadone with other opiates (such as heroin and DF 118s or other downer-type drugs such as alcohol, sleeping pills or tranquillisers) greatly increases the risk of overdose.

Take Your Methadone As Prescribed By Your Doctor
Methadone comes in different strengths – a spoonful of stronger mixture could contain 10 times the amount of methadone you are used to. Methadone bought illegally, even when supplied in a medicine bottle, could be much stronger or it could have been 'altered down', making it difficult to judge your tolerance level.

Tolerance Means So Much.
Understanding what 'Tolerance' means could be a life-saver. Think of it as your body getting used to having a drug around all the time – 'tolerating its presence'. Without tolerance, 50mg of methadone can kill an adult.

Tolerance is literally the difference between life and death. For methadone and other opiate-type drugs, tolerance builds up in about two weeks, but only if you take the drug most days of the week. No amount of weekend binges will have the same effect.

But (and this is the important point) tolerance fades as quickly as it develops. Months of irregular use will have increased your tolerance level. If you stop using regularly, your tolerance falls and a relatively small amount could kill you.

Watch Your Starting Levels.
Be cautious about dose levels during your first few weeks on methadone. Exaggerating your heroin intake to get more methadone from your doctor may get you more than your body can tolerate. **If you start using opiates again after a break, start low – tolerance doesn't survive for more than a few days.**

Safe Storage
Keep your methadone (and any other drugs) where children can't get at it. Ask your pharmacist to dispense your methadone with child resistant caps. As little as 5mg could kill a baby. This is just a spoonful.

Caution! Overdose.
Your tolerance to methadone and other opiates like heroin will fall quickly once you stop using regularly. If you decide to use again, use a lot less than you were used to. A small amount can kill you – especially if you inject drugs or use

methadone with other 'downer' drugs such as alcohol, tranquillisers, sleeping tablets and heroin.

26/6/06

Picked up Paul on my way in, intending to have a meeting with everyone to gear ourselves for the coming ten weeks before Ludlow. But only two turned up, Andrés ill, Kate's leg too bad to come, Chris in court having a review, so only Andy B and Dean – and Andy B is always pretty semi-detached at the best of times. In fact he has a cunning plan to get off gear which he explains to me:

What I'll do right, is to cut out the gear and have a smoke or two – just at night like – and perhaps the odd drink. I was at a wedding the other day see and I noticed these people going out the back and went out and saw that they were having a smoke. So I joined them and I liked that. I was off me head mind.

This is at least better than his last wheeze for getting off gear which involved illegally buying ampoules of methadone and injecting it between his fingers.

Paul really wants a full-time job on the project. He asked me if I could help him get an allotment at Leominster and he is doing courses in tractor driving. He seems completely positive and empowered. I said that the point of times like these was to store strength for the bad times that would surely come. All their ice seems awfully thin.

We did go through the motions of planning for Ludlow Food Festival – what to sow, what to nurture, what will not last, when to kill the pigs (not till Christmas), when to kill the lambs (soon and store, trying to sell them as halves – go round the visitors last

Wednesday and get them to take them). Should we sell meat at all at Ludlow, etc., etc.

Finally did a little work, digging up all the garlic and weeding. I went off to drop Paul home and then bought diesel for the tractor, a battery for the electric fence and some rabbit wire for making drying racks for the garlic and onions.

At lunch Fred from Zambia came to visit via the charity Harvest Help that I did a Radio 4 appeal for. He was charming, besuited, collar and tie, and fascinated with the detail of how we handled the soil. He showed us pictures of his few acres at home, twenty miles outside Lusaka, and his house made from bricks that he made from his soil and his seven children that ate when he produced food. Everything done by hand with a mattock. He asked for a photograph of me and a piece of chard which grew unimaginably more vigorously in our polytunnel than his at home. A man could live off just two leaves like this, he said.

I thought of the food we threw away every meal, deemed not even fit for the pigs. A family could live off the scrapings of our scrapings.

All his talk was of building and maintaining soil fertility and the unimaginable labour going into that. We have lost that in our heavy mechanised west. Lost the lie of the land. We bully it into submission. Andy Trim has it and, I guess all good farmers, be they biodynamic, organic or conventional. Nurture the land and it will nurture you. So obvious and yet so wilfully ignored.

We strung galvanised rabbit netting right across the Dutch barn and piled the garlic onto this so that they can dry. There were four wheelbarrows full.

The pigs got out on Saturday and are now in the old pig paddock and love the grass and companionship. Quite a lot of time was spent leaning on their fence or talking to and about them. They inspire sociability and it is a shame to have them hidden away in the hedge – although that makes ideal conditions for them.

234

Rocky very quiet all day – everything very low key. I take this to be a comedown after the Open Day last Wednesday. We have to let things settle and then build back up again. Find that energy again.

26/06/06

On the 21st this month we had a open day. we had a few famales came now from the gropp Rocky and wife (angy) came Tony + Jack and wife (cath) we had a bar, B,Q Tony +jack cook on the BBQ I walk the MAGISTRATS COURT round the farm and the pig sheep + plants and veg's we are growyng. I had a Good time I Didnt hear what half they said but I Did well hope I Get my hear aid soon. so my problem's solved +monty never had a silence time that day.

   thank you.

Andy B

PS Good luck.

On Wednesday we had the open day in the morning we got things ready for the people and family to come and see the project, my Girlfriend & Son Cam to the farm, with my mother and stepfather to see how I am doing. thanks to rocky, monty, Jack, Tony all made my famly more than welcome. And for me, helped a little to Build Bridges Between me and my mother, thankyou again for everyones time and help to make this project to work, and for me it has helped me so much, I know if it wasnt for this project I wouldnt have come this far. Thank you

Dean

27/6/06

Delivered wood chipper back to hire place and was eyed up by man standing in the store. I avoided eye contact and went about the business of form filling although saw him plucking up courage to speak to me. It turned out that he was one of the owners and had read the stuff in the paper and wanted to make a donation of tools to the project.

See, he said. I've got it down on my list of things to do today. Ring Monty. It's meant to be. He asked what we wanted and I said everything. Anything. Although slightly held back by my middle-class nicely brought up desire not to be seen to be greedy.

He said he would put together a pallet of tools ready for us. It felt like Christmas.

Bought a cold chicken and rolls for lunch and went over. Only two turned up again, Andy B and a new guy, Steve. He had been done for selling heroin in Leominster but was not a user nor on a script (although had only been clean for nine months). Seemed saner and fitter than most. Andy B as ever, away with the fairies but good to have around.

27/06/06

only I came and a new person steven we planted more plants on field eg collerflower. cabbage. swede. its a ongoing day not feel with it cause no one from the group is hear it very dead. hope more tomorrow will be here. I thing it not worth coming if just one person is here. the wether is Dull their's no birds singing or flying the chickens are Quiet. the sheep are hiding the pig's are nosey and No wind and no sun. Its seem it going to rain 'what a shame'!?

by

Andi B

I left them with Rocky and Jack planting and weeding after I had picked a tray of veg to take to the farm shop. When I got there Paul was making the yard good. I asked him about Steve – who had said he knew Paul. Paul said he didn't know any dealer called Steve. The only Steve's I scored off are in prison.

Paul looks brown and well. But he went to the dentist yesterday and waited until 5 p.m. until he was told that no one would see him. The dentist had a cursory look and told him to come back at three tomorrow when he would take out seven teeth.

Seven teeth! Andrés is having five out this week too which have abscesses to the bone. Andy B is due to have four out.

You get used to their decrepitude – not least because they are all so stoical about it – but when you see someone fit and healthy you realise how disastrous they are as physical specimens.

Went home, ate a biscuit and then went and guiltily brushed my teeth.

I am so tired at the moment. The fact that I recognise this is at least a start. But can't sleep much and overwhelming sense of a mountain to climb. Sarah says this why they (the family) always tread warily around me about the time of my birthday. I do recognise the pattern. I always have a strong urge for a rest or holiday and it is never possible – although I also see that the biggest obstruction is me. Increasingly see working in television as incompatible with any healthy life. Overload.

28/6/06

My father's birthday. He would be ninety-one although has now been dead for twenty-three years.

Went over at lunch time and found a much brighter more lively atmosphere than the last few days. Met new bloke Shane, from Kington, Herefordshire who seemed fine. Also visitor who had arrived unannounced looking for work having read about the open day in the paper. Tried to discourage her without wholly brushing her off.

Shane disappeared whilst we were all talking. Where's he gone I asked. He's up in the field working.

Working? Rocky said. That's unlike him.

Later on someone pulled me to one side and said that he had gone off to the loo to use. He came out with a bloodstained arm and blood on his T-shirt at the spot where it had rested against his chest as if using whilst seated. Seemed a bit tenuous to make what amounted to a serious accusation but I guess we are all jumpy about these things. It is the one absolute taboo here.

Andy Trim had to go but left his seeder and myself, Andrés and Dean used it to sow a huge amount on the raised beds that were all prepared. Ten times quicker than normal hand method.

Dean had taken yesterday off because he was tired. I am sure he was genuine in this and the surprising thing is not that he did it – a bit floppy – but that the work of Monday tired him so much. Popey looked haunted and desperately thin. He is moving house tomorrow to a shared house as opposed to a sheltered flat. He has been genuinely ill and has to have five teeth out tomorrow. He said that he gets 'really really lonely. Terribly lonely. Then I walk around desperate for someone to talk to and I just meet all the users and have to listen to their shit.' He pulls a face that is both deprecating and full of despair.

Andy B is buzzing around, daft as a brush but full of energy. This is the third day in a row he has been here – the first three consecutive days ever. He is now bossy, annoying and, as ever, rather endearing with it. It does him good.

I talk to Rocky about Shane. Rocky has already spoken to him. There is no evidence but Rocky points out to him that it can mean only two things. Either he is using or someone dislikes him enough to try and convince us that he is using. He apparently promised to come clean and stay clean whilst here and to come two days a week.

With new people coming in we have to keep re-emphasising the ground rules, keep building again from the foundations.

Chris is in hospital with the abscess in his arm. Kate is trying to get a fortnight in hospital. Yesterday Paul said a friend of his had two weeks in hospital and it was great. Got his abscesses sorted, got his methadone and was put straight into rehab when he left. Did him the world of good.

David told me that there had been a steering group meeting last night. Someone pointed out that a couple of days ago two men had cut an old man's hedge down the road and then gone in and told him that he owed them £100. Very frightened, he gave them the money in cash and they fled. Apparently the word is going around that 'one of our group did it'.

This is depressing on two accounts. The first is that it shows that the minute a crime is committed people accuse our lot. The second is that no one has begun to think it through. Our lot live miles away, have no transport, no equipment and absolutely no local knowledge – i.e. don't know who is old and infirm. They are almost the last people one would suspect. Apparently no one has gone to the police. This makes it worse as it keeps the whole thing clouded by suspicion and lack of openness.

28.06.06

Today was crap could have been better but I've had worse by being on my own but if I work with others it will be much better I need help.

Andy B

Good day again, got a lot done, feed the pig, And did a lot of seeding with Andreous and Monty, Did some weeding again.

Good Dinner getting more weight on me cant wait till nexted Monday

Dean

Today has been hard. But when Monty came after Dinner things got better, have seeded lots of raised beds Have got to get a grip and buckle down – think positive

Andrés 2006

July 2006

03/07/06

Today I watered the veg and made myself a cup of tea (it
bloody HOT) so I felt like shit cause it drains energy out of me!
but had a wicked time this weekend got recked But who cares
if it Dont included smack.

Andy B

The open day was really good! I had a lovely day! My Dad was
really proud of me + my cousin.

Kate
PS went really well

04/07/06

Hot day have done what we could have enjoyed myself must
try and get on track.

Andrés

10/7/06

I was away in Italy filming for a week or more. Came back
late Friday night, birthday on Saturday and managed to spend
three hours topping our orchard after opening fête. Sunday

was transmission of 'Desert Island Discs' that I recorded month ago. I included one song for the group. 'Road' by Nick Drake: fabulous guitar work – deceptively simple based around a basic E chord with the open G tuned down to E. I had no expectation of them listening to it. Radio 4 is not their natural home.

It turned out that a couple of them heard it but showed no great interest. This is partly because they don't find it that interesting. I'm just a bloke who does telly and radio type stuff, none of which really appeals or applies to them. There is also their intense parochialism. They would have been much more impressed if I had appeared on Radio Hereford and Worcester. Come to think of it I have never heard any of them talk about music at all, let alone express any interest in buying it or going to see live performances.

Everything growing. Piglets getting out and about and then scampering back to Mum. Vegetables growing and baking in the heat. Lambs great woolly louts, bigger than the ewes.

In the afternoon I went to Worcester to a Care Trust meeting. The upshot was much support for what has been achieved and backing for a new site near Worcester as well as maintenance of the Rock. The Trust agreed to extend the lease until 31 March to give me time to set the charity up and that will then take over the lease.

In the end it all boils down to funds. It costs about 150k a year to set up a site and run it. Perhaps easier to say an initial 100k plus 500k over five years, allowing for amortisation of capital costs. That will be for a core group of 6–8 people, permed from a maximum of twelve. Ten would be better. Probably twelve people might pass through it through a year, spending an average of 3 days a week for six months, learning skills, getting qualifications and getting on the road that will see them through, so it works out at about 10k per person. That is very cheap compared to any other option. But it needs security of tenure and some long-term funding.

10/07/06

Worked hard today, I do not no what has been wrong with me these past weeks but I am trying to snap out of it. Once I'm at the farm I enjoy working.

Andrés 2006.

11/7/06

Tuesday at the site all day – buying wood, bin bags and canes (for scarecrows), bread and pies. Kate disgruntled and unsatisfied, Andrés suffering from toothache – he had been to the dentist the other day who took out three teeth in three minutes. I commiserated with this but he would have none of it:

He was great! Young, like. Ever so friendly. Said if it hurt to tell him and just breathe deeply. I liked him.

I was given an envelope addressed to me at the Rock. It was from someone in Norfolk who had heard 'Desert Island Discs' the day before and ran a trust fund. He was suggesting we apply to it as they had money to spare. Ha! I think that is the first letter that I have ever had offering me money without asking anything in return.

We planted and weeded and tied up the tomatoes in the tunnel. Everything quite smooth and well oiled except for Barrie, who is resolutely dislocated and unconnected. He gives away nothing. However he drove the tractor and turned the compost heaps. I ask him if he is still using and he says not. Kate, sitting next to him, shook her head in disbelief.

245

I ask him why he only comes one day a week. Why don't you come twice a week? Three days would be even better. That will give you a chance to get involved, see things through a bit more.

I'm on something else on Wednesdays.

Come on Monday then.

Can't come on Mondays.

Why not?

Mondays is my chill day. It's *my* day.

What for?

He gives a little smile, Just stuff.

Rocky smiles. What's her name, Barrie? Husband away on Mondays?

11/07/06

I've had a good day today I enjoyed myself but I ent felt like myself today I dont know whats wrong but I should be OK by next week

Barrie

17/7/06

Popped over at lunchtime on the hottest day of the year so far to see how things were going. Walked into the mess hut and was instantly handed a steaming plate of mince, our potatoes, our courgettes and beans. Kate, Andy B, Andy Trim, Andrés, Steve, Shane, Dean, Tony, Lou (temporary voluntary worker) and Rocky. All seemed at ease with themselves except for Dean who was a bit withdrawn. It turns out that his girlfriend has told him that he needs to get a job and this is upsetting him. It seems that everyone connected with this lot sees them suddenly make progress after so many years and then wants to accelerate it, to push them on.

My daughter says her friends saw the article in the *Hereford Times* and some came up to her and said What's your dad doing bringing junkies into our countryside. I told the group this.

That's well out of order Kate said. Fucking cheek. They should leave your daughter out of it.

Kate's script is down to 15 ml a day. This from 60 last autumn. She reckons that she could be clean by Christmas. A whole string of negative testings now. I do my usual thing of asking each of them how the tests are going. My experience is that if they have negatives they are only too eager to tell me. Any hesitancy implies a positive test. Andy B just smiles when I ask him. He is still using.

But mainly I'm drinking now. I picked up this girl right – or tried to till her uncle stepped in. She was up for it mind but she went and told him and that was the end of it.

What do you mean – told you that if you touched his niece with a bargepole he would have you?

The conversation was along those lines yeah. She came home with me but nothing happened. Nice bloke though. Still gives me work.

Popey had been to the dentist that morning and had three false teeth put in. He ate his lunch without a twinge. Happiness all round.

The place had rhythm. It worked. We talked about the Ludlow Food Festival and what it meant. I asked them for commitment in attendance and work and they seemed happy with the prospect. The truth is that they don't care that much. It is too remote, too other. From me too. We were play acting a kind of bonding.

17/07/06

What a hot day but we still got a bit done we must get on the ball about ludlow food fest.

Andrés 2006

Good day razzin about on tractor to bloody hot to work but good for the suntan.

Steve

18/7/06

Spent the day at the Rock. Stopped at a healthfood/wholefood store to stock up on fair trade tea, coffee, soap etc. Reminds me of shopping in the late seventies. But I don't see this as a retrogressive thing – rather that the whole counter culture thing was right all along. It all comes around.

Fairly small turnout – Andrés, Dean, Barrie and new girl, Sam. She is local and seemed terrified but was nice and keen. Her daughter's name tattooed on her arm. Wouldn't tell me what she was on her order for.

It was blisteringly hot all day so that restricted what we could usefully do but nevertheless everyone eager to get on. The lambs had gone to Griffith's the butcher at 7 a.m. and are – apparently – all presold which is a relief. The ewes restless and bleating all day. Barrie and I hitched up the rotavator – with much cursing and fiddling – and he rotavated the raised beds in the old pig paddock, Andrés showed Sam around and Dean and Rocky watered and weeded. In fact most of the day was spent watering and weeding in some form or other. Barrie and I turned compost with tractor and fork – it has rotted down well and we now have four good bays of it. But we need about 40 tons so will have to buy a lot in.

Letter from a local woman whose grandson was an addict for many years. She offered her services in any capacity – to cut sandwiches or just be a grandmother to some.

That's fair enough Andrés said. That's very good indeed.

Beth came at lunchtime accompanied by a photographer and journalist who wanted an interview with me for the Ludlow Food Festival mag. Lots of posing with piglets and potatoes.

A good lunch of chicken, courgettes, French beans and mashed potatoes. Barrie ate two sausages.

I never eat white meat me. I know it's healthy but I won't.

Give it a try Barrie.

No. I don't like the look of it. It's no good. I won't try stuff I don't like.

Sam refused to eat anything at all. Dean ate sausages and the veg and Andrés ate everything – including eggs, sausages and chicken.

I ask Barrie what he does on his day off but I know the reply. I am just prodding a stick through his cage.

Nothing.

What sort of nothing?

Nothing, he smiles. Just nothing. I sleeps mostly.

I ask what sort of job he would like.

Night shift.

Are you a night person?

No. But I can't get up in the morning.

What time do you normally get up?

Four o'clock.

I don't bother asking a.m. or p.m.

What time do you go to bed?

Last night it was eight because I knew I had to get up to come here. Sometimes I rests in the afternoon too.

He has a smudgy tattoo on his upper arm – no picture but a collection of random or very faded marks. What's that Barrie?

I dunno.

What do you mean you don't know?

What I say. I don't know nothing about it. I was drunk and then when I woke up it was just there. He smiles again.

Given how much he seems to sleep the mystery tattooist had plenty of time for the job.

Barrie is exceptional in this but the truth of heroin is that it is mostly about nothing and lost time.

I talked to Dean too, who is under pressure to get a job. Dean is keen on becoming a cowman and working on a dairy farm. Although Rocky pointed out that this is on the basis of a one-hour visit, he did talk enthusiastically about it. But he said that he still felt fragile and was worried that, under pressure, he would use again. For someone like Dean, who is in his mid-thirties, there is no personal or social system to fall back on when things get tough. Heroin has negated all that and is the only thing – literally – that he knows. It means that you have to rebuild from the base up and create a foundation within themselves that they can rely on when things go pear-shaped. To push them out without is almost inevitably going to end in failure. They know this of course and it worries them a lot.

Dean is the gentleman of the group and radiates an old-fashioned decency. However he announced today that he had three sons by three different mothers.

I can only fire off boys he says.

He smiles his impossibly clean, false teeth grin (as far as I can gather he has a complete set of false teeth). Dean is short and slight and looks much younger than his years. Come to think of it most of them look very young. Maybe they are. Maybe I'm just getting old. On his arm is tattooed 'ghost' because he used to be so pale, but when he says this about his sons he suddenly is roguish and virile.

My brother's the same. He can only fire boys. I've got a son of seventeen, a son of fourteen and my lad now who's nine.

Do you see them?

I see the seventeen-year-old. He's still at school 'cause he's a bit special. Got an age of seven or six. I reckon he will still be at school for a few years yet. But he's doing really well. He's all right. I see him every few months or so. It's strange because the local users in Swindon who know me from my drug days all speak to him. That's confusing for him.

Do you see the fourteen-year-old?

No. I last saw him when he was nine. His mum don't want him to see me. She won't have anything to do with me. I left her for her best friend. But I never had a child with her. Then I left her for my missus and I been with her for eleven years.

After lunch I sat with Andrés and asked him about his life. This is what he told me:

Andrés Pope

I was born in Spain on 21 May 1974. My father worked for Thomson's Holidays and we lived in Benidorm and then somewhere in Majorca. I can't really remember any of that although I was a model for Ladybird clothes! My father left when I was about four. Never had any contact except for when I saw him for a few hours when I was twelve. I have a sister two years younger than me and we were brought up by my mum who returned to England – the West Midlands – when my dad left. My mum did everything she possibly could. Brought me and my sister up. She worked as a secretary, took us on holiday, did all the decorating – everything.

I didn't feel that I fitted in well. I wasn't bullied. I just didn't fit in. People used to take the piss. Like in those days everyone had really short shorts. Coming from Spain I had long shorts. People thought it strange. I went to Hagley Secondary School. It was Roman Catholic. I was brought up a Catholic and still am although not a very good one. I've lapsed.

I started playing truant and generally misbehaving. I wanted to fit in, wanted to be acceptable. But I chose the wrong crowd to fit in with. If you take drugs with the people you are hanging around with you certainly fit in. I was expelled from Hagley when I was fourteen. Not for anything in particular – it was just a culmination of things. They wanted to get rid of me.

I didn't go to another school. I had home tuition but I first went to prison when I was fifteen. Theft. I was taking hard drugs by then. Heroin and amphetamines. I injected straight away. There was this huge attraction to injecting heroin. It was dark and mysterious. Everyone was taking drugs but only the real hard core injected. This was very attractive to me and I thought it was really cool. I was fitting into the inner circle. I used to think the Happy Mondays and Shaun Ryder were pretty cool. I now think Bloody Hell!

It's surprising how quickly drugs take over. I wasn't like other normal people. Mum was really, really upset. But heroin is a great one for getting rid of guilt. I would say I was sorry, but sorry is just a word.

Prison did scare me but it didn't scare me enough. Not enough to stop me at any rate. I didn't use in prison at first. But as time goes on you meet people outside and the contacts are made. There was a time when I would use anything that I could get my hands on but it was mainly just heroin.

I had a slight problem with crack in 1998–99. Quite a big problem with it actually. Anything and everything just goes on it. So I went to prison and dried out and just used heroin.

I've been to prison seventeen or eighteen times. The longest was eighteen months. The 7th June 2005 was the last time I was in prison. This last thirteen months is the longest I've been out of prison since I was fourteen.

Some of the time I lived at home, sometimes dossed with friends. I've lived on the streets quite a few times – for six months in 1998. Last year I *asked* if I could go to prison – it's a chance to clean up, get three meals a day, work, read, get sorted. Like a health farm really.

This place has changed my mindset. My behaviour is completely different. I look at the bigger picture now instead of the instant. I haven't used since the end of January, beginning of February. I realise that when you have a relapse you've got to get back on that horse and go back into battle. The cravings get easier bit by bit.

I have abused alcohol but I'm learning that I can't do that. Instead of one lager watching telly I'd have ten or twelve or as many as I could get my hands on. I last had a pint last Thursday in a pub. I don't smoke cannabis or take ecstasy. I don't agree with it. They're all drugs and all illegal. They all get you into trouble.

I've still got a lot of work to do with myself mentally and physically. I don't know what the future holds. I don't think I'll ever have a family or an apartment in London. But hopefully I can lead an enjoyable and quiet life.

19/7/06

I took over a Magimix, Parmesan, pine nuts, olive oil, grater and scales and we made pesto from the basil in the polytunnel. When I got there there were Rocky, Andy Trim, Lou, Sam, Steve and Shane and Beth, Kate, Andrés and Dean arrived half an hour later having been to the poultry place in Church Stretton to order some rare breed hens. Far too expensive but interesting and entertaining.

I also picked a large bowl of our raspberries (the best raspberry year I have ever known) which we had for pudding – following a very good fish pie made by Beth. We eat well nowadays. Sam ate nothing again.

The great baskets of basil were picked and bought back to

the mess hut and we set up a chain gang with one lot stripping the leaves, one grating cheese, one preparing garlic from our harvest, another weighing everything up (Sarah's recipe from *Fork to Fork*: 6 oz basil/2 oz pine nuts/3 fresh cloves of garlic/ ⅓ pint olive oil/teaspoon Maldon salt/4 oz freshly grated Parmesan) and I whizzed it all up and added the oil before another lot ladled it into storage containers. This way we did a lot in a short time.

It was the first proper cooking of our own produce that we have all done together and felt fun and slick. Everyone took a big tupperware pot home and there was some for the freezer and a big bowl for the fridge. Everyone seemed excited by it save Shane who said he didn't like the smell or fancy any. But Shane is cheerful so this was said without the usual reproach. He is thirty-five – looks twenty-five (It's funny how we all look young innit? Heroin is good for that), comes from Kington, heavy tattoos, affable and straightforward, almost hearty. Not the archetypal user.

Kate asked me if I wanted to read her diaries. Only if you want me to I said. Yeah, I don't mind. Which ones? Do you want the good stuff?

Of course. What do you mean?

Well I got ones when I was shoplifting a lot and taking gear and crack all the time and others when I was clean for eight months.

That's a long time to be clean I said.

Yeah well I met a girl didn't I. That's pussy power.

Perhaps you need to meet another girl I said, meaning to keep you clean, but realising that it sounded salacious.

Chance'd be a fine thing. I'm not fussy. Blokes or girls.

Steve is from the north and his accent places him instantly as different from the rest. He is clean and not on a script. Consequently is healthy looking with a good physique. Despite the shaven head, rings, tattoos etc. he has a real twinkle in his eye. He lives in a hostel in Worcester. What's it like? I ask.

Shithole.

I thought that was a bail hostel said Andrés. You're not on bail are you?

They all know the workings of the system inside out. As it happens Steve is not on bail but has another year on his order and nowhere else to live. I ask him what he wants from that year.

I want a job man. As soon as I can.

He is more than ready for one. But a drug dealer with a criminal record, living in a bail hostel, has hardly any chances.

Letter from someone moving to a smaller house and offering us her gardening tools – over thirty items. Stuff is flowing in.

Temperature clocking thirty-five degrees on the thermometer.

19/07/06

O what a day Myself Kate Dean and Beth went to get rare chucks and we went to a rair breeds farm. And made PESTO

Andrés

23/7/06

Went over to the Rock with my son Adam to pick up Paul's parents' barbecue. When we got there the doors of the mess room were open and no barbecue. Eventually found Paul by the pond collecting tiny frogs from the grass. Apparently David had taken it over for them yesterday.

It was the first time I had seen Paul for weeks and he looked in good nick. We stayed and chatted with him for a while, saw the pigs, wandered round. It was very peaceful – a hot summer's morning in the middle of the countryside. Complete quiet. We must help Paul get some qualifications – he could easily get a train to Hereford and the sixth form college, which apparently has a good agriculture section. Must look into that.

24/7/06

Went over for lunch.

What's for lunch Rocky? Meat and two veg?

No. Got a change today. Two veg and some meat.

In fact it was courgettes, yellow beans, our potatoes and mince from the farm shop. Not inspired on a day with the temperatures in the low thirties but more than adequate and friendly. Dean and Steve were the only ones of the main group but Paul had come for the day too. Lou, Rocky, Tony and Andy Trim were there too. Andrés came later after his court hearing – which apparently was a big success. Andy B was apparently unwell and Chris Smith contracted MRSA when he was in hospital for his abscess on his arm. Kate was at the dentist.

Andy B's order finishes on 10 August so theoretically he is free to leave then. I also learned that he has never been to prison because of his deafness. This marks him out from the others – and why I have never been able to find any court record on the internet.

I asked them about prices and quantities of heroin. As ever they all perked up when talk became drug specific. The detail of ritual never fails to fascinate them.

A 'bag' is a fifth of a gram and costs £10 locally but can be as little as a fiver in a big city – especially if you buy some quantity.

How many bags did they use a day. Five? Six? They all laughed. Paul said that when he was dealing he would use an eighth a day. (An eighth is 3.5 grams or 18 bags.)

Was a bag a hit? More dismissive laughter. Paul said:

I used to use a teenth often enough.

A teenth?

Sixteenth of an ounce; 1.75 grams.

Dean said that he has seen hits of up to 2 grams in one go. Ten bags. Mind you, he said, I've seen people go over on half a bag. Depends what you are used to.

I liked the 'go over'.

So what were they spending?

Hundred pounds a day easy said Steve.

And the rest Paul said. Then there's crack.

Ah well Steve said. With crack you just spend everything you got.

Steve and Paul said that they would have a syringe by the bed so that they could use the minute that they opened their eyes.

Half a gram in the morning, first thing, set me up said Steve. Then a bag every three hours or so. The thing about gear is that you can pace it. If you haven't got much or no money you can spread it out like. But you got to have it.

What about crack?

Crack's all right until you have that first pipe. Then you got to have another. And another. There's no stopping then. But if you keep away you can resist it. Not like gear. With gear you always want it.

Rocky said that a serious user needed to steal £50,000 income a year to finance the habit. Could be a lot more.

So where do they sell it?

You'd be surprised, said Paul. Not so much by where but by who.

The people who keep the drug industry going are the receivers said Rocky. The same people who turn their noses up at drug users are happy enough to buy the stolen goods.

Yeah when they know you're a user they shit on you too, Paul said. You take them fifty quid's worth of stuff and they offer you ten. Now off you go and buy your drugs with that they say. If you won't take it then they tell you to bugger off.

257

And the violence of big cities is getting to places like this said Rocky. Country places are becoming more and more affected.

We switched topics with barely a flicker to the future of the pigs and decided that we should buy a six-month-old boar – not Tamworth but preferably Gloucester Old Spot – put him with the pig for a litter and then when he has done the dirty have him off for bacon. The current piglets can be fattened for Christmas pork and Miss Piggy kept for future litters. The one that she would have with the Old Spot boar would introduce vigour into a rather incestuous set-up.

So we went and moved the pigs – which took ages in the sun because they really, really did not want to leave their home in the ditch, which is lovely and shady, woody and wet. Eventually we got mum across to their new home by the pond (they had spent the morning making it) and after an hour the last piglet was taken – literally kicking and screaming. Once there we decided to leave the mother overnight and then split her off in the morning.

25/7/06

Boiling hot day. I stopped on the way at the healthfood store to get cans of organic drink as requested and tubs of local ice cream. Cupboard love. They – Andrés, Dean, Barrie and Sam, with Lou, Jack and Rocky – were there before me and out moving the sow back to her proper quarters. She delighted to be on her own and not having to feed the six monstrous babies any more.

Andrés and I started fixing the fencing for the piglets – which was extremely ropey – when David Reeve appeared to say that a topper had arrived. So Barrie, Andrés and I unloaded it and fixed it onto the tractor. This is a brilliant development because it means that we can cut the grass in the field – which is awful, just stems – to encourage the good stuff to grow. Then, when we get some decent grazing we can have some cattle. So the topper is a key to introducing the calves that I have wanted on the project since last autumn.

Barrie then spent the entire rest of the day doing the topping, riding round and round the field in decreasing circles. As Rocky said – if half the police force in Worcester could see him now they would never believe it. It did rather surprise me. He had never sustained more than about half an hour before.

Dean spent the day mowing with my mower that I brought in, cutting all round the raised beds and along the line of the rabbit fence to stop it earthing on the long grass.

Then Andrés and I went back to fencing the pigs. He told me that he was pissed off with his National Trust job. He had felt pressurised into doing it by the probation service but it was not right and he would much rather be on the farm. He felt as much sorrow as anger at probation. They haven't got a hope he said. Three of them have over two hundred to look after. But he felt he had made a false move with his NT job and was stuck with it otherwise it would look as though he was ungrateful or a shirker.

But, he said, I looked up what you said about communes. I found something about one in Peru I like the look of. Helping children. And another in south London and one in Malawi. Peru would be good.

I had been thinking along the lines of Gloucestershire or perhaps as far afield as Devon, so was slightly surprised at this. But I said I would help if I could, although my contacts in Peru are a little limited.

He can't come in tomorrow because has to go to court. Wrongful arrest.

It's dragged on for ages. It's a pain in the arse. I wish I had said I had done it now.

Did you do it?

No, of course not. But if I had said I had it would be all over long ago.

Then lunch – our own home-made pesto and pasta. Dean

disappeared to be sick halfway through then came back to say that last night he had met a friend in Worcester on his way home.

I'm going to Droitwich to score he had said. Want to come?

I said no. I wasn't doing that. But I chatted to him at the railway station while he waited for his train. We was in the waiting-room and he started skinning up. I looked over and saw two Asian blokes snorting coke off a cigarette packet. Then fuck me if a bloke and a bird came in and he didn't start rolling a joint too. I thought fucking hell, what hope is there if I go to a railway station in rush hour and everywhere I look someone is taking drugs!

But at least you didn't use.

No I managed that all right. But it's hard if you can't get away from them. Four years ago my missus and I moved out of Swindon to get away from the drugs. On the day we moved I had my last hit thinking that's going to be it. The next morning we walked into the middle of Droitwich, just a short way into the town – village really. I was rattling but OK. I saw this bloke outside a bus station and asked him if he could score for me. He said that he was on his way to score and could get me what I wanted. There you are – took about five minutes in the middle of a tiny town where I knew no one. Hopeless.

Oh yeah Droitwich, Andrés said. You'll have no problems finding drugs in Droitwich.

If people are using and you're with them you gotta use too haven't you, Barrie said.

I said You don't *have* to. That's what getting clean is all about.

The only answer is to remove yourself, Barrie said. Go somewhere else. It's all you can do.

I've never been done for drugs Dean said. Been done for all sorts of other things to *get* drugs but I never been done for drugs.

We went back to finish the pig pen after lunch to find not a single pig penned. They had got out, and were away exploring our neighbour's field and it took all afternoon to round them up, get them back – where they promptly got out again, squealing with pleasure – and then fix the fence whilst the piglets slept soundly in the mud, exhausted by their games. A Red Kite flew over, low, tilting and tipping its wings. The first I have seen over the farm.

The BBC director said it seemed to be a happy, relaxed sort of day. I realised that this was the best measure of our success. It had been relaxed and happy – yet lots got done. Weeding, topping, harvesting (lots of purple and yellow beans), eating our own pesto, fixing fences, mowing, talking, dealing with animals. The prospect of a relaxed and happy day three months ago – let alone six months ago – was impossible.

Relaxed and happy is a fucking triumph.

Major Review of Voluntary and Community Sector
25 July 2006
A significant review will take place over the next few months by Home Office (HO) and the Department of Health (DH), which will look at the part the Voluntary and Community Sector (VCS) plays in the delivery of the National Drug Strategy.

Government recognises that the voluntary sector has already played a crucial role in reducing the harm drug misuse causes to individuals and communities. An independent, robust, financially sustainable, representative and supportive structure for those voluntary organisations engaging in delivery of the Drug Strategy is critical to maintaining this progress.

As part of the development work on this review DH and HO have worked closely with Drugscope. The Consultants Cordis Bright have been appointed to undertake the following:

Identify and map relevant organisations involved in second tier activity.

Consult key stakeholders on current and future needs in relation to second tier functions, e.g. representation, policy, support.

Review best practice in second tier activity across the voluntary sector and highlight key learning points for the drugs sector.

Draw conclusions and put forward recommendations in relation to: (a) roles and responsibilities of the second tier; (b) relationship with Government; (c) desired outcomes from and priorities for second tier activity and appropriate accountability.

The project will involve substantial consultation with a number of stakeholders from across the field, including the VCS. It is hoped that those contacted will engage with the project which starts immediately and will finish in the autumn.

www.drugs.gov.uk, 25 July 2006. Crown copyright © 2006

26/7/06

Stressed and irritated is clearly not so successful. Angry email from Tricia this morning complaining that some idiot from the project had removed stakes from outside their office yesterday . . .

I apologised meekly by email and promised immediate re-imbursment. It seems that when I asked Barrie to get the fencing posts from the chicken pen he went to Tricia and David's chickens, looked around and saw some leaning against the wall. The fact that they were nowhere near the chickens and that there were signs with similar stakes attached clearly did not work its way through his brain. When I asked him if they had come from the chickens he assured me that they had.

We had a long meeting at home with an adviser into setting up the charity – all good stuff although a huge amount of work to be done. But it all has to be set up with maximum speed because of the telly programme. We must be ready by then.

When I got to the project just after lunch David was remonstrating with Rocky because someone had broken a branch on his chestnut tree in the middle of the field. It was Barrie again. When called over to explain he said that 'the tree hit the tractor' when he drove near it. We pointed out that it was more likely that the tractor hit the tree and that the driver of the tractor had some responsibility if not cause of this. He apologised but clearly could not see he had done anything beyond the normal wear and tear of work. I took him down to clear up the fallen branch and repair the torn wound on the tree.

So not happy landlords. There is an essential problem which David and Tricia's remarkable generosity of spirit and their tolerance in nearly all matters does obscure. They live in the same space, feel ownership of every aspect of the site and yet there is a commercial lease. The two things are wholly incompatible

As I was leaving, into the heavy evening, a hobby skimmed across the vegetables with bent-back scythe wings. I had never seen one before but there was that process of elimination – too sharp winged and swift-like for a kestrel, too slight for a peregrine, too big for a merlin – and the sudden jolt of recognition – like seeing someone very famous on the street or tube.

A kite and a hobby in two days is, despite local problems, happy is relaxed is a fucking triumph.

28/7/06

I went and talked more with David and Tricia, to get their viewpoint of how things were going.

David and Tricia

David: At first I was very involved setting up the mess shed, not least because we had a vested interest where the changes were permanent so I wanted to have a hand in it.

Tricia: You enjoyed it.

David: Absolutely. It was interesting working with them. When they were constructing something they felt a sense of achievement that they probably hadn't felt before.

I tried to pair people up because teamwork was something that they didn't understand. Working in pairs was a start. Mind you some people wouldn't work with anyone else at all. It was a long slow process. You'll remember better than anyone that it was a miserable winter. Seemed to be permanently wet. That was testing.

As we finished the shed there were less things to see tangible progress on and in parallel with all that Tricia was cooking the meals. To start with the remarks and rejection were difficult – to say the least.

Tricia: I was asked by the probation service to produce good solid nursery meals, which is what I did, and they were rejected.

David: It was a slightly – what's the right word? a slightly *corrosive* process to start with but we brushed it off to a degree but as it went on and on and Tricia was not well it clearly became too much.

264

Tricia: I understood that they might learn to share food and enjoy it but after all that rejection – not to say the hassle getting the money for it – I thought bugger it. I got cross.

David: And Tricia's Lupus got bad again.

Tricia: Lupus was discovered when I had a stroke in Africa and was totally paralysed down one side. Locally I had a jolly good GP and consultant in Cheltenham and Lupus was diagnosed. Sometimes it can be undiscovered for years. You can be absolutely fine then – like the last few weeks – hardly able to move because it flares up.

David: Our perception of drug users is that they are incredibly self-centred and arrogant. Anyway what with that and Tricia not well we decided that it was too much stress in our lives. So we stopped the meals.

Tricia: It wasn't worth the effort. At that point we realised that we were too involved with the project and other things in our lives were being impinged upon. Every five minutes the doorbell would ring – can we borrow this, can we borrow that.

I was also extremely angry in March when we found out that they were still using drugs. When we raised this we were told yes of course they are still using. And they are very proud of it. We would overhear them talking about it.

We understood that the public were told that no one would use and if they did they would not come back. I was *extremely* angry about this. I felt betrayed – by the management, not the kids. I do understand that it is extraordinarily difficult to get off any addiction. You can't do it. It is too difficult. But the probation service said that they would not be taking drugs and it was absolute bollocks. I'm still cross about it.

David: It was a turning point in our direct approach – we withdrew a bit after that – but it didn't lessen our support for the scheme. In the light of this experience it needs to be spelt out very clearly what their drug use is and is likely to be. I am sure that everyone at the public meeting believed, like us, that they would not be using drugs. Anyway we had decided to pull out by then.

Tricia: I watch the failings that happen and get incandescent about the rubbish in the yard – the way that tools get thrown down. The way that the hay was just taken without asking. Little things like that make me very cross.

David: It was all part of our experience with the project. Mind you I was more used to it because I was a soldier. Our problems have always been with the running of it – not the principle. It is not a blame game but a matter of learning how to do it.

Tricia: It doesn't help that everything is done for them – they are taken everywhere. It contributes to their self-centredness. I really do think that life should be a little harder sometimes. I feel that everyone drives hither and yon, sorting them out and they just sit there. They play on this.

David: You need to impose responsibility on them – but find a way of putting that responsibility on each other.

Tricia: They don't talk to each other . . .

David: Things have improved a lot. They now work together much better. But they are not a team – they don't talk together and plan together. I would suggest a number of mini-team tasks. In Operation Raleigh each day a different person was in charge of a little project. This begins to inculcate a sense of organisation and leadership. Slowly they would get the idea of organising things for the project – and themselves – and begin to organise their lives a bit more. Paul for example is a good thinking lad and has come on leaps and bounds. It can be done.

Tricia: What does the future hold? Well I hope that in spite of all the failings and stutterings that it will have enough impetus to go on to other groups. There is absolutely no reason why not.

David: I see two main difficulties. One is money. Where is this going to come from? It really needs government funding. Somehow it needs to be built up. And secondly the business of direct management and leadership of the project. You need a full-time person who is probably young and probably seven days a week. Someone coming out of agricultural college and is young and enthusiastic and wants to do it. Therefore this needs to be promoted as a national scheme.

From Hereford Times, *27 July 2006, Thursday:*

Herefordshire coroner David Halpern has called for more help to be given to drug addicts after they are released from prison.

He made the comments after hearing of the death of a 23 year old Leominster man, Andrew Cuthbertson, from a drugs overdose weeks after being released from prison.

Mary Cuthbertson said her son had a history of heroin addiction but had been determined to kick the habit when he came out of prison.

. . . Dr Simon Elliot, a toxicology expert, said in a report that blood samples showed morphine and heroin use.

He said that the ability to tolerate the drugs depended on usage and after a period in prison people often became less tolerant.

Karen Cuthbertson, who found her brother (dead) said despite being a heroin addict he was a good man.

'He tried to come off the drug but it was really hard,' she said.

Det. Sgt Dugmore said . . . he would like to see more help for addicts who he described as 'especially vulnerable' when they came out of prison.

'He said people re-entering a society of drugs were especially at risk because they had reduced tolerance. There was a danger that the amounts that they had taken before would prove fatal.

'I have seen this many times,' said Mr Halpern. 'What is needed is the political will and money to provide special help.'

He later recorded a verdict of accidental death as a result of morphine poisoning.

MPS SAVAGE GOVERNMENT'S 'AD HOC' DRUG POLICY

The Guardian, *Monday 31 July 2006*
James Randerson, science correspondent

- More addicts than ever before, says chairman
- Dereliction of duty by advisory council alleged

MPs have mounted a savage attack on the government's drugs policy, denouncing it as 'based on ad hockery', 'riddled with anomalies' and 'not fit for purpose'.

They have also challenged the basis for the ABC classification system, saying that the harm caused by drugs should be separated from criminal penalties.

The criticisms come in a report from the parliamentary science and technology select committee published today as part of an inquiry into how the government uses scientific evidence in policy making. It describes as 'dereliction of duty' the failure of the government's expert committee, the Advisory Council on Misuse of Drugs (ACMD), to alert the Home Office to serious doubts about the effectiveness of the system. 'If the government wants to hand out messages through the criminal justice system then let it do so, but let's not pretend to do it on the back of scientific levels of harm from drugs because clearly that isn't the case,' said Phil Willis, chair of the science and technology committee. 'The only way to get an accurate and up-to-date classification system is to remove the link with penalties and just focus on harm.'

The investigation – entitled Drug Classification: Making a Hash of It? – found no evidence that the sliding scale of classification deters users from taking the more harmful drugs. 'We have more drug addicts today than we've ever had and we have more people using class A drugs than ever . . . the classification system as a device to reduce harm to individuals and society has failed,' Mr Willis said.

The report does not offer a detailed alternative to the current arrangements but says criminal sanctions could be better linked to the level of

> criminality surrounding particular drugs, and that
> penalties could make a clearer distinction between
> individual use and dealing. The report falls short of
> calling for personal drug use to be decriminalised.
>
> The MPs also criticised the government's 'opaque'
> approach to changes in the system and the way in
> which the changes often appear to be a 'knee-jerk
> response to media storms'. Neither the Home Office
> nor ACMD chairman Sir Michael Rawlins was
> available to comment.

31/7/06

Went over at lunch. Dean, Andrés, Paul, Kate, Rocky, Jack and Andy Trim there. Sat down to a plate of our boiled ham, yellow beans and a salad of our lettuce, cucumber and tomato – these last two the first picked (although I have been eating them at home for the past 3–4 weeks). The others had spent most of the morning gathering the piglets back from various scattered fields and fixing the fence – again.

We discussed a potential new site that the charity would raise the money to buy, which Andy Trim had been to see. He was very pro it but I pointed out that we had nothing in the bank and my own funds were running perilously thin. Money had to be raised and with that endless legalities and bureaucracy to go through. But everything seems possible.

Someone said that Chris Smith was recovered from MRSA.

He used this morning but he's OK said Kate. His arm's better. But he's a real bad crack addict. Real bad.

Kate looked a bit rough. Her script was now reduced to 15 ml.

I had a negative on Friday. But I never did no gear over the weekend. I went to a festival over the weekend and I took every drug in the world except crack and gear. Coke, pills, grass – you name it I had it. That's maybe why I feel a bit rough today. At two in the morning we shone our mobile phones and within one metre was every drug you could think of. It's bad really.

But I should be on Subutex on the fifteenth.

That's good, I said. Really good. You should be proud of yourself.

Yeah I know. She didn't seem convinced.

Maybe you should be completely clean I said. No drugs at all. No booze. Completely clean.

Yeah I know. Perhaps. Who knows?

August 2006

1/8/06

Cool and showery. The first day for weeks when a shirt has not felt quite sufficient. Low turnout today, just Rocky, Sam and Dean and me. Barrie was too tired to come, Kate had to have the dressings on her leg changed, Andrés was in court (re a crime he vehemently denies doing), Steve had an appointment made by the probation service and Andy B is not very well.

It was nice. Slow, gentle and intimate. We also got quite a lot done. Dean and I turned the compost heaps – Dean proving a cautious but extremely competent tractor driver compared to the macho styles of the others and Sam and I sowed a lot of seeds in plugs and seed trays. Also tomatoes pinched out and tied up, animals all fed and much weeding done. The rain has made the fat hen grow everywhere. Fat Hen (*Chenopodium album*) is a powerful weed with prolific seeds – each plant can produce up to 100,000 of them – but the pigs love it and it used to be a harvested crop in neolithic times.

Dean came out of prison for the last time four years ago and this is the longest he has been out of prison since he was sixteen. He is now thirty-seven. He is good company and has a quiet positivity that is infectious. It will be a real loss when he goes.

01/08/06

Today is tuesday only me Sam And Rocky And Monty today. been a good day had a Drive onthe tractor today and turned the Composs with monty. planted Another line of veg today hopefully

forthe stall at the ludlow food festavale it will Be good to See our
food Being injoyed By other's hope-fully things will go fine.

Dean

We had a visit at lunchtime from Gloria, a local grandmother who
wrote to me after reading the article in the *Hereford Times*. Her
son was a user for many years and was in and out of prison but is
now clean. She is more than happy to cook, write letters or just chat
to the group. She ate a lamb chop with us (and our spuds,
courgettes and onions) and agreed to come back next Tuesday
to begin by making lunch for us. This was the first truly local
person who has volunteered to help and as such, is a big moment.

Rocky and I drew up a list of successes and failures. The latter
first:

- Lee and Paul (Razor) both back in prison. But both only came
  to the Rock a couple of times and neither has been since last
  September.
- Chris Spires in prison. We didn't do it for him. He didn't want
  to be clean but also only came perhaps ten days in total over a
  couple of months.
- Wayne arrested for theft the other day and waiting to go to
  court. Wayne only came here a handful of times and the last
  two or three was unable to work because of kidney failure and
  an embolism in his leg. I haven't seen him at all since early this
  year.
- Tim Green (whom I only met once – refusing to get out of the
  car) is in prison for dealing.
- Martin is dead.

The truth is that all six of them probably had a total of twenty days'
attendance between them in twelve months. Increasingly I feel that
the order should have built in a goal of three days a week with a
minimum of two days a week attendance for a minimum of three

months – preferably six. Any missed days have to be made up by the end of the month. Regular attendance is the key. At the moment other parts of an order have to compete with coming to the farm.

The success stories are:

- Chris Davies off gear and methadone, in a job, holding it down, still with his fiancée and looking for a flat.
- Chubby working (casually but regularly) and having driving lessons.
- Paul Mellor working, off gear, in a job and focused on getting off his script.
- Adam Harrison still working and clean.
- Andrés Pope the longest out of prison and least drug use since fourteen.
- Kate script reduced to 12 ml (from 50 in January) and falling.
- Shane, Andy B, Sam, Dean, Steve and Barrie all attending regularly, not committing crimes and largely not using.

We come out ahead I think.

2/8/06

They were all there when I arrived plus Gloria and a big cake that she had made. Beth preparing lunch. Andrés and Dean and Sam working with Andy Trim in the field. I took Andy B off to have a chat. His order is due to end on the tenth and as I am away next week this could be the last time I see him. He has had a virus and said that he had lost three stone in a week. I'm eight stone now.

I'd take that with a pinch of salt but he did look thin. I have spent many hours talking to him over the past year but it has always tended to be one-sided. Because of his deafness conversations can be tricky. He answers questions obliquely at best and wildly, weirdly at a tangent most of the time. I want to nail down his life story, to sit him down and quietly try and put a version of his life down on paper.

Anyway, this is what he told me.

Andy Breakwell

I was born on 11 June 1979 in Evesham. My family comes from Malvern. My dad was a labourer and I got two sisters and a brother. I'm the second with an older sister. Mum and Dad divorced when I was three and I got my stepdad when I was five. I love them all. It's only what the drugs done that made them fall apart.

I was born deaf or it was very low when they done tests – they knocked me nerve bone and I had a bit more hearing. I had a hearing aid.

I didn't learn to talk till I was seven.

I went to a special school for handicapped people when I was two and a half, because I couldn't communicate or anything. My parents never treated me no different. They always let me get away with things because I didn't hear much. I didn't want to be left out. I just wanted to be like anyone else.

I went to Defford Primary School and they had special teachers. Very nice school. Then they put me to Pershore when I was eleven. I had to redo all my stuff again because they had no records. Because they made me feel dumb I never bothered doing it. That's when the school made me feel left out because I was doing different to everyone else.

All them years I felt left out. I got bullied because I was deaf and that. I played with hardly no one.

I started to get into trouble at thirteen. Little things. I wanted to be with the other people. That's when drugs started. Marijuana, drinking cider, pills, acid. I liked the atmosphere. I didn't like the drugs using but I liked the way that people treated me. I did it for the friendship and that's what I shouldn't have done.

278

I started using gear when I was fourteen, fourteen and a half. I injected straight away. People would give it to me when I was off me face. No one told me anything. I didn't know nothing about it. When I was an addict then I knew it was wrong. *Then* I knew I had a problem. And it was too late.

I kept it quiet for seven years. I never got into trouble. Police, family didn't know I was using. They thought it was drink. I used to drink as well so I smelt of drink. They had their suspicions but because I was hard of hearing they thought that I would learn from my mistakes.

I left school at sixteen. Whilst I was at school I would inject in the morning and smoke dope during school time. I got a job painting powder paints. Six months. Then went on a farm. Six months. Then in 1998 I went to Doncaster College for the Deaf. I learnt to weld, everything about cars. Lots of things.

I was still using but it wasn't a problem. That's when I slowed down to two bags a day. One in the morning and one at night. Before that I was using heavy. I paid for it by selling dope. You see I could mix with deaf and with ordinary people. Deaf and dumb people would keep asking me to get gear and crack for them. I would get 750 quid's worth but it would only cost me £350 so I kept the difference. They was happy – I was happy.

Yes it was in Doncaster that I had a child.

I left in 2001. After Doncaster I got a job welding. I left after nine months and got my habit back full bore. I was using 17–35 bags per day which for me – 'cause I was dealing a bit – was £60–£120 a day.

I was living at my mum's after Doncaster but then they kicked me out. I don't blame them for that because me attitude was changing. I had that fight with me stepdad. That was the pills.

I lived on the street in Worcester for two years from 2002 to 2004. I was shoplifting and stuff. Dealing. I got others to do it for me because I couldn't hear what they was saying.

Did loads of crack. Crack has been more than heroin what's damaged my life. First took it when I was thirteen. It wasn't

279

cheap back then. You could buy a tenner's worth. It would be £40 in gear. I've taken it ever since.

I got into trouble with the law. I had no criminal record before 2002. I was first arrested when I started shoplifting in 2003. Then I got in more trouble with shoplifting, burglary, money by deception. It all added up. They gave me this order August 2005. Twelve months. That's when I decided to change. Sort myself out.

I got my first script back then. 90 mls. I'm still on 90. I'm still using all the time but I don't use every day now. I did till last Christmas. Then every few days. I'm now using about every 6 days. I've got 3 clean tests now.

I've been ill. Had liver trouble cos all me immune system is knackered.

I keeps doing that step where I can leave it alone for a short period but for some reason I keeps going for it. Nine out of ten times it's mostly when I'm bored. That feeling kicks in at night-time. It seems to be a problem. It seems to be a fixation. Something inside you seems to build up. You seem to miss something. Injecting without the drug doesn't work but not injecting doesn't work either. Is it the drug or the injecting? I've tried smoking it but that's no good. I've tried all sorts of stuff.

I reckon as soon as I've got that hearing aid I'll feel more independent. I'll feel more confident.

I'm going to say to meself every week I don't use gear I'll buy myself two driving lessons. That's the deal I made with myself.

This farm has been very, very helpful. That's a fact. It took me a year to build up confidence to know what I got to do. I wish I did it at the beginning of the order not the end.

I want a job. Because I *can* work. I've got to get off this drug. I don't want to lose me meth and the testing will still go on. That's good.

I ain't much of a dreamer – I don't want fast cars, flash houses or nothing. My dream is I just want to be normal. All I want is to have me own home, have a job, have a family and live normal.

I just don't want to be different. I been different for so long.

End

There is no end of course. No grand finale. By the time you read this I hope that Rocky has his new site near Worcester. It would be great if I had found another, permanent site to buy and the wherewithal to pay for it and set it up for the foreseeable future. Perhaps we will have a decent rabbit fence in place. I would forgo all of these things if I knew none of the group had used since writing these words.

We went to the Ludlow Food Festival and, for us at least, it was a triumph. Over three days we sold everything that we possibly could harvest, made serious money for the project, met a huge amount of people and the entire group performed brilliantly.

But at the time of writing – late September 2006 – two of the group look like going back to prison over the next week, Katie is due to have a major operation on her stomach to have an ovarian cyst the size of a football removed (which the doctors mysteriously failed to notice for over a year – not that I am for a minute suggesting that this oversight might be connected to the fact that she was a known drug user and criminal who didn't receive the treatment that a 'normal' person might have expected) and others are still struggling. There is no happy ending. Just the best we can that will see us through.

The orders come to an end of course and one of the biggest concerns that we have developed over the past year or so is the lack of support for users when their DTTOs finish. In theory they are free to go and do whatever they choose. In practice some of them, like Andy B, still get tested which helps keep them focused on staying or getting clean. There are other – but precious few – people like Rocky in the country, who follow up their charges and keep in touch. But as a society we don't know what to do. We are all hopelessly out of our depth.

Governments, large institutions and big businesses are all ill-equipped to deal with this problem. They are too blunt and clumsy. They cannot see the wood for the trees.

But I believe it comes back to the very simple premise of this scheme. It is down to us as individuals. It is, after all, our problem. It is personal. We have to own it and face up to it. It stems from lack of connection, lack of responsibility, lack of identity. Lack of love.

It is simply a matter of caring for ourselves, for other people and for the physical world we share.

The essence of this is thinking small. It must be modest in ambition. Governments act in broad sweeps and whole communities and cultures, let alone individuals, get lost between the cracks. Small acts of kindness often achieve much more. In the end none of us can do very much, but if lots of people do a little it just might be enough.

The last couple of years in which I have set this thing up and got it going have been exhausting, deeply distressing and as rewarding as anything I have ever been involved with. There has been much laughter, albeit often as a result of humour as black as pitch. There has been terrible sadness. I have nothing but admiration for the people that I have got to know through working with them, particularly in the probation service and police, all of whom, day in and day out, work against impossible odds for precious little reward.

The best thing of all has been to spend a year or so with this particular group, whom I have grown deeply fond of. They are all decent people who got in a mess and yet, showing guts and toughness that most people cannot imagine, are struggling to get out of it. You will read this book and pass by. Their struggle stays for the rest of their lives.

*　　*　　*

I have set up a charity, called The Monty Project, which has three goals.

1. To purchase and run a site that can act as a blueprint and centre which can be visited. This site will produce organic vegetables, fruit and meat and share it with the immediate community through farm sales, local markets and a box scheme. It will be small in size and modest in ambition. We have found that 4–6 people is the ideal number at any one time drawn from a group of about eight.
2. To help and advise others wishing to set up and run sites in their own communities.
3. To create and support training and educational opportunities for addicts to help them get employment.

This involves liaising with the local police and probation services, social and health services and local and central government. But the essential factor is that instead of issuing edicts from on high and imposing them, each local community applies its own guidelines in a way that works best for them. By definition there can be no hard and fast rules for this.

I would like to believe that we can have scores of sites all over the country, ranging from a back garden in a terraced house or an allotment to hundreds of acres on a hillside. Each one will be small and low-key. The very strength of the idea is that it is infinitely flexible to the specific demands of each location. I am absolutely certain that if we can just sow the seed of good food, hard work in the fresh air and the whole culture of caring for something else, be it animal or vegetable, and then sharing it with other people within your own community, then we shall be doing something to benefit everyone involved. But to change the way that people think, you must start at the bottom – at ground level.

The Monty Project

Details of the charity 'The Monty Project' may be found at www.themontyproject.com

Appendix

Morphine

Morphine Morphine
What made you so mean?
You never used to do me like you do
Where's that sweet gal I knew?
My Morphine will be the death of me

Gillian Welch, 'My Morphine'

The project did not begin as a drug thing. It was conceived as a way of repeat offenders getting out of ingrained attitudes and habits through connecting to the earth, the weather and their local community. I realised that drug use would be connected to this but had completely underestimated how closely drugs and persistent crime were linked. Spending time with the group made me realise how drugs dominated their lives. They were vague and careless about most details but immediately concentrated on the specific when it came to drugs. In the literal sense of the word entranced, they were fascinated by them and in particular by heroin.

So I did a little research into how heroin became such a prevalent drug.

It begins in Germany in 1805 when a German chemist first synthesised morphine from opium and it was soon advertised as a new wonder medicine that was non-addictive and could even be used for the treatment of opium dependence. About 1850, the hypodermic syringe came into use. Thousands of soldiers in the American Civil War came home addicted to morphine given to them to ease the pain of their injuries. In 1874, again in Germany, heroin was first made from morphine – again it was advertised as non-addictive, this time as a substitute for morphine.

Non-medical use of opiates was not an offence in the UK until after the First World War but doctors were still allowed to prescribe them. But by the 1960s all but a few specialist doctors were stopped from prescribing it.

The mid 1970s saw the beginnings of illegally manufactured 'Chinese' heroin from Hong Kong. In the mid 1980s the number of users of heroin and other opiates increased dramatically, particularly in inner city deprived areas. This type of heroin was originally produced for smoking rather than injecting and came from the so-called Golden Crescent countries of Iran, Pakistan and Turkey.

If statistics bore you or mean nothing then look away now but they are worth enumerating just to get an idea of the scale of the modern heroin trade.

In 2005 global opium production was estimated at 4,620 metric tons of which 4,100 metric tons (89 per cent) were produced in Afghanistan, with the street price of heroin at £50 per gram at June 2005.* The resulting value is around 230 billion pounds (1 million grams × 4,620 × £50).

That 4.62 billion grams is broken down even further. The smallest unit of heroin is a 'bag' which is .2 of a gram and which is selling at £10 in the provinces as of 2006, although it can be as little as half that price in the big cities. Regular users might well start the day with half a gram and then have about .25 of a gram every three hours. Heavy users – such as most of the group on the project – can easily use 3.5 grams a day, especially if they are

* Source: Druglink survey, Sept. 2005.

dealing and have access to it – which amounts to 15–20 bags a day. The average 'problem user' (the official term for people such as our group – i.e. people who finance their use through crime) will get through between five and ten bags a day.

A regular user will therefore need around £100–£1,000 per week with an average of about £500 (NEW-ADAM survey, Bennet, 1998; 2000; 2001). My group told me that you can get through '£100 per day easy'. Police suggest that to make this amount of money from stolen goods you must multiply this by three as stolen goods make on average a third of their normal value.

The most common crime committed – by a large measure – is shoplifting. Some of my group have become expert at this and will shoplift to order, stealing, for example, specific outfits to supply their customers for special occasions with the right sizes and colours etc. But in the main the shoplifting is opportunistic, random and pathetically trivial.

Taking a conservative estimate of 250,000 'problem misu-sers',* as the unwieldy state jargon describes them, each with a habit costing around £15,000 p.a., you have thefts amounting to retail worth over £10 billion a year – and it doesn't take much pessimism to use government figures to double that estimate.

Then there is the cost of dealing with that crime. This includes police arrests, police custody, custodial bail, court appearances and prison. On top of that there are the insurance and security costs to the companies and individuals on the receiving end – all costs which eventually filter through to the tax payer.

Finally, there are the huge social costs of looking after drug misusers, including GPs, dentists (all heroin and crack users have terrible teeth), Accident and Emergency, hospital residency,

* Home Office figures for 2000, published in 2002 by the Drugs, Alcohol Research unit of the Research, Development & Statistics Directorate. NHS figures published Sept. 2004 states '250,000–350,000'.

hostels, social services, probation services and benefits. None of this counts the loss to society of the skill, expertise and social input of all these users.

My non-statistician's head is already reeling. No one has tried to add all these figures up but anyone can see that it is a huge sum of money. And only the dealers are benefiting. You might argue that with drugs like ecstasy or cannabis at least most users have a good time for their money but heroin offers nothing but release from unimaginable craving. These pages show just how little pleasure is involved in heroin addiction – and none of the agencies dealing with them from the health service to the police have the resources to cope. Everyone loses.

Home Office figures for 2000, published in 2002 by the Drugs, Alcohol Research unit of the Research, Development & Statistics Directorate, show the following:

Number of regular older users of class A drugs 1,091,000–2,182,000.
Class A problem users in England and Wales 281,125–506,025.

The report from 2002 was the first real attempt to provide a survey of the economic and social costs of class A drug misuse. Costs associated with problem users are: GP, accident and emergency, hospital days, mental health services, state benefits, criminal justice system, police arrests, acquisitive crime, police custody, court appearances, prison.

The government figures from 2000 show that for problem drug users total economic costs range from £2.9 billion to £5.3 billion (it is a huge range but vagueness and huge variations dog all figures in this field), with a median of £3.5 billion per year, i.e. £10,402 per user per annum. Add total economic and social costs and the figures rise to £10.1 billion–£17.4 billion or £35,500 per user per annum. This happens to be the current annual cost of keeping an individual in prison.

Methadone

Like morphine and heroin, methadone was invented by the Germans, this time in World War II as a synthetic analgesic after they lost their access to the Turkish poppy fields. In 1964 research done by the New York City Health Research Council's Committee on Narcotics discovered that different opiates had quite different effects on users. Heroin and morphine produced the familiar fixated dependence whereas methadone, once administered, enabled users to take an interest in other things and lead normal lives. By 1970 there were 1,000 cases of patients on methadone treatment in New York and by 1973 there were 80,000 Americans enrolled in methadone programmes.

It has a longer half-life, or effect, than heroin – 15 to 30 hours – which means that the user is more chemically and metabolically stable. Oral methadone works within one hour of dosing, with peak effects experienced between two and six hours after a dose. The group say that the correct does taken in the morning will last them through till lunchtime the following day – i.e. about thirty hours. Then with the advent of HIV AIDS methadone became increasingly used by doctors because it could be taken as a liquid and thus avoided the use of needles.

Methadone has great virtues: it is safe to administer, has a long half-life, reduces crime and increases health. Its dosage can be accurately regulated and reduced. Death rates on heroin are sixteen times higher amongst injecting users than their non-injecting peer group. Methadone users are only twice as likely to die.

However it is a powerful drug. It is extremely hard to kick, causes dry mouth, constipation, lack of concentration and engagement and a host of other physical symptoms. It is still opiate addiction. There is a strong argument for supplying clean heroin rather than methadone on the grounds that it is easier to come off heroin and most of the problems associated with the drug are to do with its supply and method of use rather than the effect on the user.

As with everything to do with this subject, it is almost impossible to find accurate statistics about methadone users. The National Drug Treatment Monitoring System collects monthly data for each client of structured drug treatment services prescribed a script – but does not include details of what that script is. There is also a database of all prescriptions written by GPs which measures the volume of substitute prescribing but not the number of individuals prescribed to.

The most accurate figure available, from 2005, is 90,000–100,000 individuals in England receiving scripts with approximately 75 per cent receiving methadone. (Doctors can still prescribe heroin if it is considered more suitable.)

There is no budget for this nor specific accounting. In other words no one knows what it costs. I have been quoted a figure of £3,000 to £5,000 per person per 'episode' of use but the caveats that went with that quote mean that it should be regarded as a very rough guide. The Royal Society for the Encouragement of Arts (RSA) says that the government spent £226 million in 2004 prescribing methadone to addicts; at £4,000 per user that would suggest just over 56,000 users which squares with the 75 per cent of the 90,000–100,000 figure quoted above.

The West Midlands Drug Treatment Programme

The West Midlands region has a population of 5.3 million with a central conurbation of Birmingham, the Black Country, Coventry and Solihull accounting for 2.3 million of that figure. Herefordshire and Shropshire come within the region but have a population density of only 90 people per square kilometre which is one of the lowest in the UK.

Historically the investment in drug treatment services in the West Midlands has been one of the lowest in the country with only just over a third (36 per cent) of the funding in 2003/4 coming from health, social care and criminal justice agencies. Where, one wonders, did the vast majority come from?

The NHS gave figures in September 2004 of an estimated 250,000–350,000 problematic drug misusers in the UK in 2003/4. Of those, 33,100 were from the West Midlands region. That figure should be set in the context of 22,165 for the whole of London. A total of 12,986 received specialist treatment in the West Midlands in 2003/4. This figure excludes users in prison.

In 2003/4 the Department of Health funding for drug treatment was £27 million. This is set to increase to £53 million in 2007/8. Social services, police and probation expenditure is in addition to this.

All government pronouncements are frosted with infantile 'targets'. How about: 'the NOMS (National Offender Management Service) will support a number of the Government's high-level targets. These include the following:

- *to reduce the harm caused by illegal drugs (as measured by the Drug Harm Index).*
- *to reduce crime by 15 per cent – and more in high crime areas – by 2008.'*

I like the 'high crime areas'. You have to grasp at any shard of humour you can find when wading through these figures.

Withdrawing

There is no moral judgement to be made about addiction. The fact that heroin is illegal and involves a huge rate of crime to finance does not make the addiction itself wrong. It is no more 'wrong' than anorexia is wrong.

The hardest thing for any addict to deal with is that despite the fact that, by definition, they cannot help themselves – no one else can. Anyone who claims to have the perfect treatment to get someone else off drugs is lying or ignorant. The addict will only control their addiction when they want to and are ready. Then they must do so every single day for the rest of their lives.

Addicts seem to be mostly born not made although some things, such as nicotine, coffee, heroin or crack cocaine, are highly addictive. I have every single box-ticking element of the addictive personality yet do not have a shred of addiction in me. Some people get lucky.

The consensus seems to be that prisons are riddled with drugs. Drugs, rather than the cosy 'Porridge' unit of tobacco or snout, are the measure of currency and power. One of my group was asked, wide-eyed, by a new addition to the filming unit, if there was much male-rape in prison.

> *Yeah, of course there's some of that goes on. But nowadays they're mostly after your drugs. They hold you down and scrape out your arse with a spoon.*

Arguably the UK's prison system can only be maintained with heroin acting as a sedative. Clean them up and they would explode. Yet most of the addicts that I have talked to over the past couple of years withdraw from heroin use in prison, especially if they get into a Class 'C' prison. They use it to clean up in every way. They withdraw, feed properly, read, work, study and get their acts together. Yet without exception they all started using again very soon after coming out.

This raises a whole range of questions, most of them baffling. Who would want to go through all the rigours of reforming themselves only to return to their old ways so soon? Why? Is it because they are all a thoroughly bad lot and ungrateful to boot? The glaring truth is that prison is a wholly unnatural environment that works best for them as a rest camp. More than once I have heard them refer to it as a health farm. When you are living on the streets, having to steal £500-worth of knick-knacks to pay for your habit, your body is becoming appallingly unwell and violence, lies and rejection attend every waking hour, then the comforts of prison might start to outweigh the horrors of a group of lads with a lascivious smile brandishing a small spoon.

The other factor is that Cold Turkey – usually referred to as 'the cluck' or 'the rattle' although 'the cluck' shows how rarely modern youth comes across a turkey in full gobble – is not pleasant but not *that* big a deal. Dean, one of the older members who started in spring 2005, said that when he started using he would do so for a week then not touch it for a week.

I must have been rattling all along but I never noticed. I just thought I had this horrible cold I couldn't shake off along with night sweats.

All of them say that they can lock themselves in their bedroom and rattle for a few days till they feel well enough to function. But, having watched a number of them rattle when they have had their methadone scripts suddenly reduced or if they have forgotten to take it, it is deeply unpleasant and seems to be akin to a nasty bout of flu, involving weakness, vomiting, sweating, aching bones, diarrhoea and neuralgia. Not good.

The systems vary from person to person and circumstances. It has long been noted that rattling seems to be milder in police custody – and it would follow from that, in prison. The greater the availability of relief, the greater it seems the physical distress of withdrawal.

Heroin suppresses the activity of the adrenal gland via the control centre in the brain. When this suppression is removed extra adrenaline is produced and it is this that accounts for many of the unpleasant withdrawal symptoms. If you have ever had to make a speech in front of a large group of people or take part in an important sporting event you will be unpleasantly familiar with the symptoms of loose bowels, weakness, sweating, dry mouth and extreme weakness and fatigue – all of which disappear the minute you engage with the activity concerned.

There has been much debate whether it is better to have rapid dramatic withdrawal which is bad for a few days and usually completely gone within a fortnight or so – the locking yourself in a bedroom route – or slow gradual withdrawal so that life can carry on during its process. This latter method usually means cutting back methadone at the rate of about 10 per cent every few weeks over a period of six months to a year.

But on one thing everyone agrees. It is not getting off heroin that is difficult. It is staying off.